"There is nothing more powerful to dramatize an injustice like the tramp, tramp, tramp of marching feet."

Martin Luther King, Jr., June 7, 1966, at a rally in Memphis, Tennessee, during the March Against Fear

THE LAST GREAT WALK OF THE CIVIL RIGHTS MOVEMENT AND THE EMERGENCE OF BLACK POWER

Countless supporters joined James Meredith (center, wearing pith helmet and grasping walking stick) for the final hike of the March Against Fear, June 26, 1966, to the Mississippi State Capitol in Jackson, including civil rights movement leaders Martin Luther King, Jr. (left of Meredith, arm linked with wife Coretta), Stokely Carmichael (right of Meredith, wearing overalls),

ANN BAUSUM

WASHINGTON, D.C.

FOR THE MARCHERS,
THEN, NOW, AND ALWAYS.

—AB

CONTENTS

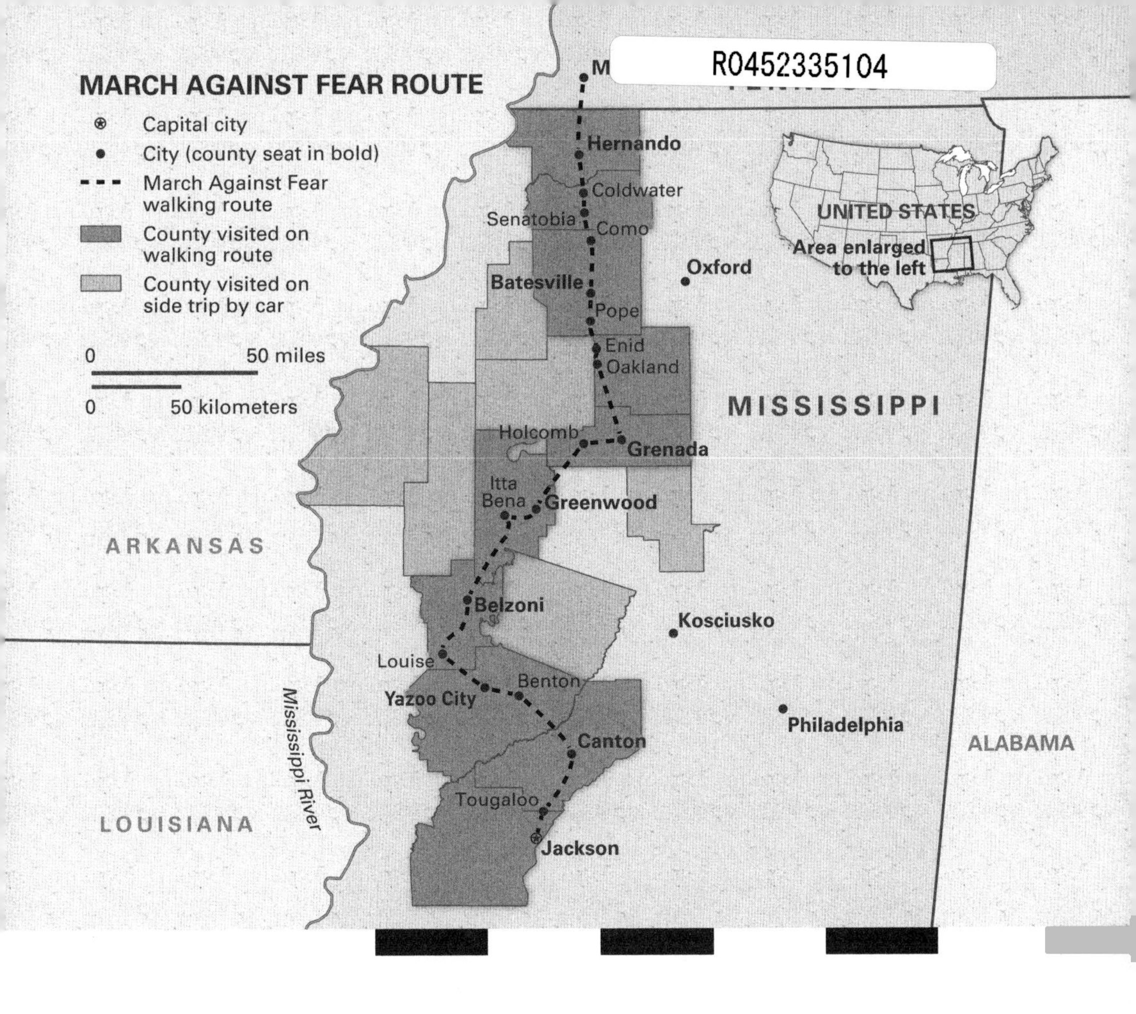

A NOTE ABOUT LANGUAGE

Readers will travel through history with this book and encounter examples of language old and new, respectful and hateful. In my text, I use the terms "black" and "African American" interchangeably and with equal respect. The widespread use of the word "Negro" in quotations from historical source material should be viewed within the context of the times as a term of respect, too. Racial epithets of that era remain no less offensive today, but they are a part of the historical record and are presented in quotations from the period without censorship.

—Ann Bausum

PROLOGUE

A TREMOR

BLAM!

One minute James Meredith was walking along a rural road in Mississippi, two days into an estimated two-week-long journey to the state capital of Jackson. The next minute a stranger had climbed out of the roadside honeysuckle and started shooting at him.

The first blast from the 16-gauge shotgun spewed tiny balls of ammunition toward the hiker, but the pellets struck the pavement nearby, not Meredith himself.

Undeterred, the gunman fired again.

BLAM!

Some pellets found their mark.

BLAM!

Shotgun pellets from the third blast penetrated Meredith's scalp, neck, shoulder, back, and legs. His hiking companions seemed frozen in place, transfixed by shock and unable to react to the sudden threat.

Meredith had cried out in surprise when the shooting began. Then he, like those walking with him, began searching for cover. He dragged himself across the pavement, trying to put distance between himself and his attacker. He collapsed on his side, sprawled upon the grassy shoulder of U.S. Highway 51, his blood oozing from multiple wounds into the red soil of Mississippi.

The penetration of countless tiny balls of shot through his skin left Meredith moaning in pain. "Get a car and get me in it," he implored the others at the scene. An ambulance arrived quickly, and within minutes Meredith was being raced back along his hiking route, bound for a Memphis hospital. Emergency room physicians concluded that his wounds were not life-threatening, although they could have been if the shooter had been closer or his aim more accurate.

James Meredith collapsed in the road after he was ambushed and shot in rural Mississippi on June 6, 1966.

Doctors shaved the back of Meredith's head and dug as many as 70 pellets out of his scalp, back, limbs, even from behind an ear, before they questioned their effort. Although only a fraction of the 450 or so shotgun pellets fired toward Meredith had found their mark, countless balls of shot remained embedded in his flesh. Yet it was so time-consuming—and so painful—to remove them, that doctors decided to leave the rest alone. He wouldn't be the first person to walk around with bird shot under his skin. Soon after, a local news reporter found a medical resident familiar with the case and asked him about the patient's condition. The doctor-in-training replied with a candor that, although shocking today, would have seemed unremarkable at that time in the South. "If he had been an ordinary nigger on an ordinary Saturday night," the man observed, "we'd have swabbed his ass with merthiolate [an antiseptic] and sent him home."

But Meredith was not an ordinary man, black or otherwise, and his shooting would have a seismic influence on the turn of events beyond his own world.

"I wanted to give hope to a barefoot boy. I was a barefoot boy in Mississippi myself for 16 years."

James Meredith, explaining one of the reasons behind his planned walk through Mississippi

James Howard Meredith graduated from Ole Miss in Oxford amid a sea of white faces on August 18, 1963. He was the first African American to earn a degree from the institution, having integrated it the previous year.

CHAPTER 1

WILD IDEAS

JAMES MEREDITH was already famous before he got shot on June 6, 1966. Indeed, his fame probably made him a target for attack, and his fame certainly accounted for why his shooting made the national news. Otherwise he would have been just the latest overlooked victim of white-on-black violence in a state where whites had used violence—and fear of violence—to secure their supremacy since the era of slavery.

At the time of his birth in 1933, Meredith's parents chose to name him simply J. H., using initials in place of a first and middle name. His family lived on a farm outside Kosciusko, Mississippi, and his parents' decision represented both an act of courage and an acknowledgment of the challenges their son would face growing up in the segregated world of the Deep South.

Even names held power then.

Social custom during that era dictated that blacks address whites by adding titles of respect to their names, such as Mr., Mrs., and Miss. This gesture emphasized the place of whites at the top of a race-based social order. Whites reinforced the subservient stature of African Americans by routinely addressing them by first name only. Whites also often converted the given names of blacks into childish nicknames that might last a lifetime. Meredith's parents chose not to give him a proper name, such as James, which could have

DATES WALKED: June 5–6 **MILES WALKED:** 28 **ROUTE:** Memphis, Tennessee, to south of Hernando, Mississippi

become a source of humiliation if whites called him Jimmy instead.

Despite his exposure to this world of white supremacy, Meredith emerged from his childhood with a remarkable sense of his potential and self-worth. Maybe it was the pride he felt because his great-grandfather had been the last leader of the region's Choctaw Nation. Maybe it was the power of those childhood initials. Maybe it was the security and independence that land ownership brought to his parents as they raised their 11 children. Whatever the causes, the result was that J. H. Meredith had a fierce determination to make something of himself.

And he had complete confidence that he could do it.

When he turned 18, J. H. added names to his initials and became James Howard Meredith; he needed a full name in order to join the Air Force. A few years before, President Harry S. Truman had ordered the integration of the armed forces of the United States, so Meredith was among the first wave of recruits to serve in an integrated Air Force. He spent most of the 1950s in the military, culminating in a three-year posting to Japan. In 1960 he returned to Mississippi, newly married, and in pursuit of further education for both himself and his wife. Initially the couple enrolled at all-black Jackson State University, but, in 1961,

Federal marshals and other U.S. security personnel stood guard to ensure that onlookers remained orderly when Meredith registered for classes at the University of Mississippi on Monday, October 1, 1962.

Meredith set his sights on transferring to one of the most revered all-white institutions of the South: the University of Mississippi, otherwise known as Ole Miss.

Ever since his teens, Meredith had dreamed of going to his home state's flagship university. Having served in an integrated military, and having heard newly elected President John F. Kennedy's call in 1961 to national service, Meredith dared to imagine integrating Ole Miss. Others had tried and failed; perhaps he could succeed. So he applied. And he persisted in claiming his right to be admitted regardless of his race. His audacity triggered a fury among staunch segregationists and led to widespread opposition to his enrollment. Months of legal battles ensued, going all the way to the U.S. Supreme Court, which, on September 10, 1962, upheld Meredith's right to attend the school.

Yet when Meredith appeared on campus to enroll in classes, the state's governor personally blocked him from doing so. The lieutenant governor performed the same maneuver on a subsequent enrollment attempt. This struggle went on for days, and, at its climax on the last day of September, local segregationists besieged the federal forces that had taken up guard outside the university's administrative offices. After dark, the mob grew

Even the use of tear gas failed to disperse a mob of angry whites who rioted at Ole Miss in an effort to prevent the university's integration. Cars set ablaze by the segregationists still smoldered when Meredith enrolled the next morning, October 1, 1962.

increasingly hostile and began attacking the armed personnel. Two observers died during the ensuing violence in a conflict that some likened to the final battle of the Civil War. News coverage of the unfolding drama ensured that Meredith gained national fame along with his eventual admission to the university. Everyone knew who he was and what he had achieved.

Meredith had exhibited unusual courage and determination during his Ole Miss enrollment struggle. He seemed unflappable. Able to endure any insult without being provoked to retaliate. Always restrained under pressure. Focused on some future spot on a horizon that sometimes only he seemed able to see. Meredith maintained that focus for the rest of his studies even though he required constant protection by U.S. marshals and other military personnel. After combining his credits from Jackson State with three semesters of coursework at Ole Miss, he earned his college degree on August 18, 1963.

The battle to integrate Ole Miss took place during the opening years of a growing movement for African-American civil rights. Meredith's hard-fought success served as one more piece of evidence that change could take place in the Deep South. By the time he graduated, the civil rights movement had grown into a national force for social justice, with multiple organizations working to break down the rule of white supremacy. The same month that Meredith graduated from Ole Miss, for example, movement leaders mounted the historic March on Washington and its culminating "I Have a Dream" speech by Martin Luther King, Jr., who had become a towering figure in the struggle for racial equality.

A cornerstone of this social justice movement became the willingness of people to put their lives on the line in the fight for change, much as Meredith had done during the integration of Ole Miss. Volunteers in the movement countered the violence of segregationists with tremendous acts of courage. They stood their ground peacefully in the midst of racist attacks, confident that love was a more powerful emotion than hate. Year after year, they persevered, whether it meant walking to work instead of riding segregated buses during the Montgomery bus boycott of 1955 and 1956, or braving violent mobs during the freedom rides of 1961, or enduring police attacks with high-pressure fire hoses during the Birmingham campaign of 1963.

Such efforts drew on what movement leaders called the power of nonviolence. Some viewed nonviolence as a strategy, a series of tactics that forced reluctant foes to submit to change; others saw it as a way of life. For nonviolence to work, people had to be willing to remain peaceful, but determined, in the face of any level of violence. They had to outmaneuver their violent oppressors and step in and complete a protest whether their comrades had been arrested, injured, or even killed.

During 1965, after segregationists murdered a black youth who had advocated with others in Selma, Alabama, for equal voting rights, civil rights leaders vowed to carry on the young man's fight by walking from there to the state capital of Montgomery, 54 miles away. King, other leaders, and their supporters made the march to demonstrate their determination to end the discriminatory practices that had kept blacks from voting in the South for nearly a century. The walk from Selma to Montgomery had become a triumphant procession that spring, lasting five days. The march's compelling demonstration of the power of nonviolence had helped to secure passage later that year of the Voting Rights Act of 1965, federal legislation which finally ensured universal access to voting in the South, regardless of race.

Meredith remained on the sidelines during all of these developments. Although he could have joined forces with the civil rights movement after he earned his degree from Ole Miss, Meredith chose to maintain his independence and to focus on his own goals. While others were protesting for civil rights, he obtained further education. First he accepted an invitation from the government of Nigeria to study abroad. Meredith was intrigued by the opportunity to see how blacks lived on a different continent, and in early 1964 he moved to Africa with his wife and young son. The following year he ended his studies as a graduate student at the University of Ibadan and returned to the United States so he could enroll in law school at Columbia University in New York City.

After integrating Ole Miss, Meredith had developed a reputation within the civil rights movement for being a quirky loner. Fiercely independent, he could be feisty and impulsive. He had a tendency to make provocative statements and to seem dismissive of the work of other activists. Movement leaders eyed him cautiously as a result, never sure if they could count on his support. Meredith kept his distance from the movement; it didn't suit his personality or his mind-set to immerse himself in such a broad campaign. He preferred to be in control.

As a military veteran, Meredith still thought like a soldier. He trusted the power of hierarchy, discipline, and military-style precision more than the power of nonviolence. He embraced the era's more traditional view of manhood, believing that men proved their worth with courageous behavior. Meredith disliked the civil rights movement's strategy of including women and children in their protests. He thought that doing so made men weak. The women and children appeared to be shields, protecting the men from attack. Shouldn't it be the other way around, he thought. Shouldn't men be brave enough to stand up for their rights on their own, as he had done at Ole Miss?

This visionary man toggled back and forth between two styles of thought. On the one hand, Meredith thought strategically. Join the military. Get an education. Start a family. On the other hand, he had outsize plans for himself, such as integrating an iconic all-white fortress of education. By combining his skills at strategic planning with his ambitious vision, Meredith had accomplished remarkable feats. Few others could have endured his Ole Miss legal battle, student harassment, and threats of bodily harm. But he had. And why?

The answer was obvious to Meredith: It was his destiny.

Meredith acted with an unwavering confidence that he was fulfilling some predetermined plan to serve as a leader for the oppressed members of his race. That sense of destiny—what he called his divine responsibility—had inspired him to integrate Ole Miss, and in the spring of 1966 it led him to set a new challenge for himself and for the state of Mississippi. This time he wanted to battle something even bigger than Ole Miss, something even bigger than segregation. This time he wanted to battle fear, the fear that pulsed through so many racial interactions in the South. Meredith, age 32, maintained that he was tired of being afraid of white people. Furthermore, he wanted other blacks in his home state to stop being afraid of whites, too. If Mississippi's African Americans could just stop being afraid, he suggested, everyone would be better off.

Meredith planned to fight fear with his feet. He'd take a walk, what he called a Walk Against Fear. That summer, after finishing his first year of law school, he would start walking in Memphis, Tennessee, just across the state line from Mississippi, and not stop until he'd reached Jackson, the state's capital, some 220 miles away. Meredith didn't see his hike as a protest; he saw it as something ordinary that anyone should be able to do. He credited his mother, Roxie, with inspiring the idea. The year before, she'd confided in him that she considered Meredith's youngest brother to be in less danger while fighting in the Vietnam War with the U.S. military than he would have been if he'd stayed at home. Her statement had shocked Meredith. Maybe African Americans wouldn't be so afraid in Mississippi, he'd concluded, if they had more control over the state's governance.

For nearly a century, southern whites had denied blacks their share of political power by denying them their right to vote. But now, for the first time since the post–Civil War era of Reconstruction, the newly enacted Voting Rights Act of 1965 enforced rights that had been granted in 1870 with the 15th Amendment to the U.S. Constitution. A year after the latest legislation, though, the majority of the state's African Americans had not yet registered to vote. The key remaining obstacle on that path, as Meredith saw it, was fear: fear of the consequences blacks might face if they chose to vote. By walking from Memphis to Jackson, Meredith hoped to inspire African Americans in his home state to become a bit less afraid. They, too, could take a walk against fear, a short walk that led to the ballot box.

Meredith speculated that the concerns of his mother and other southern blacks might be unwarranted, might be a lingering habit developed during earlier eras filled with real terror. Was their fear "just operating on its own accord"? Meredith wondered. And what about the white citizens of Mississippi? They were afraid, too, afraid that the advancement of one race meant the inevitable decline of another. That didn't have to be so, Meredith believed. He'd try to prove his point and conquer his own inherited fears by walking through his home state.

But Meredith had another reason to undertake the endeavor, too, and it came from another one of his outsize goals. Ever since his teen years, he had entertained the idea of campaigning to become the governor of

Meredith departed from Memphis, Tennessee, on foot, bound for Jackson, Mississippi, 220 miles away, on June 5, 1966. Friends and onlookers joined him for stretches of the first day's walk.

Mississippi. Two decades later, he still wanted to run for governor, but he knew he had no chance for success as long as the people most likely to vote for him were the people least likely to show up at the polls. Thus Meredith hoped his walk through Mississippi could serve two purposes. Not only might it encourage the state's blacks to become voters. It might inspire them to vote for him in a future political race.

This time, Meredith wanted his activism to be different from the confrontation at Ole Miss. He wanted no federal troops, no bloodshed, no drama.

No big deal.

That was the plan.

He couldn't have chosen a tougher place for his undertaking. Mississippi was arguably, in 1966, the most segregated, most oppressive state in the Union when it came to its treatment of African Americans. The Mississippi power structure ensured that whites controlled the governor's office, the state legislature, and local communities. Whites served as judges, and jurors, and jailers. Whites ran its school boards, elections, and voter registration.

Whites controlled the newspapers in the state and ran its most prosperous businesses. Whites dominated the farms that produced the cotton that was synonymous with Mississippi, a crop that for centuries had been picked almost exclusively by slaves and their descendants.

Meredith's walk seemed guaranteed to provoke controversy. He would be striding into a state where people had threatened his life repeatedly during the Ole Miss fight just four years earlier. The sheer audacity of a black man walking into Mississippi, head held high, afraid of no one, could only spell trouble in an era when such organizations as the terror-based Ku Klux Klan and the less violent but equally racist local White Citizens' Councils influenced life in Mississippi as much as—or more than—elected officials and the rule of law.

Despite the dangers, Meredith made the barest of plans for his trip, although he later claimed to have purchased a sizable life insurance policy to provide for his family in case someone killed him. He debated whether to arm himself. Months before his departure, Meredith had alerted local authorities of his intentions and requested law enforcement protection during his walk; perhaps he should trust he would be secure. Although Meredith had not seen himself as being devoted to the power of nonviolence, he wasn't an advocate for violence either. In the end, he dismissed the idea of bringing a weapon and decided to arm himself with a Bible instead.

Meredith set off on the afternoon of Sunday, June 5, 1966, with $11.35 in his pockets. He carried no backpack, or bedroll, or food. "There are a million Negroes in Mississippi, and I think they'll take care of me," he told the cadre of reporters on hand to accompany him. A handful of local black supporters came along, too, as did several allies who had traveled from northern cities to take part in the effort. Memphis officials didn't want to invite criticism for failing to protect Meredith if something went wrong, so a police escort joined the group, too.

The entourage departed from the historic Peabody Hotel in downtown Memphis, crossed through the city's segregated neighborhoods, and passed the gates of Elvis Presley's Graceland home, bound for the Mississippi state line. Most people along the route were friendly. Blacks waved. Whites generally stared or ignored him. A few people expressed their objections by jeering, making threatening comments, or waving the Confederate battle flag, a Civil War–period symbol that segregationists had resurrected during the civil rights era.

Meredith hiked with his own symbols, including a walking stick made from ebony and ivory that a Sudanese village chief had given him during his stay in Africa. "We shall arrive," the chief had told his American friend at the time; Meredith hoped the memory would serve him well on his new journey. Meredith wore a short-sleeved cotton shirt, gray slacks, and hiking boots on that hot, sunny afternoon. He shaded his face with a yellow pith helmet, another symbol of his connection to Africa. After covering 12 miles in fewer than five hours, Meredith reached his objective for the day: Mississippi. The state line lay just ahead and could wait until tomorrow.

He and his companions resumed their walk the next morning, Monday, June 6, accompanied once again by members of a press corps that, at the time, was predominately composed of white men. Mississippi law enforcement officers took the place of those from Tennessee as they crossed the boundary. The high point for Meredith on the second day's hike came when they reached Hernando, the first town south of the state line. Some 150 local blacks turned out to greet him, offer encouragement, and give him assistance—everything from a free hamburger to a dollar bill.

"I was ecstatic," Meredith recalled, decades later. He hadn't been sure if his walk would inspire others to be brave. Just gathering to meet him took real nerve during an era when any demonstration of support for racial equality in the Deep South could trigger retaliation from whites who controlled the region's jobs and jails. When he'd set out on his walk, Meredith had believed, as he would later state, that the "day for Negro men being cowards is over," and here was evidence that he was right.

Then 90 minutes later a gunman literally stopped James Meredith in his tracks.

“With this announcement black people across the country began crossing Meredith’s name from the list of those in the land of the living . . . They were black and they knew. Mr. Meredith had announced his death.”

Julius Lester, civil rights activist and author, recalling reactions to James Meredith’s announcement for his walk through Mississippi

“I don’t think it’s going to amount to much.”

Nicholas Katzenbach, attorney general of the United States, commenting on James Meredith’s plan to walk from Memphis to Jackson

"I think the entire incident is God's gift to the civil rights movement. We can do with it what we will. If we accept it and build on it, who knows what might come of it?"

James Lawson's thoughts for Martin Luther King, Jr., about the attack on James Meredith and his survival

CHAPTER 2

REACTIONS

OTHING ABOUT Aubrey Norvell's life appeared particularly noteworthy until Monday, June 6, 1966, when he started firing a shotgun at an icon of the civil rights era. Norvell and his wife lived in a quiet suburban neighborhood in Memphis, Tennessee. They had no children. They'd married shortly after World War II, a conflict in which Norvell had served with distinction. He and his father had owned and run a local hardware store together until 1963; in recent months he had been unemployed. No one could recall him commenting for or against racial equality, nor did he have any known connections to white supremacy groups.

After firing three shots at James Meredith, Norvell had turned to reenter the roadside underbrush alongside Highway 51. Only then had law enforcement officers recovered from their shock at his sudden attack and arrested the gunman. Norvell offered no explanation for his actions, and his motivations remained a mystery. Perhaps due to Meredith's prominence, the local judge set a steep bail for the attacker's release, $25,000, a sum equivalent to more than $180,000 today. This was more than double the typical rate for such offenses, and it exceeded the value of the Norvell home. Unless someone helped to secure his bail, Norvell would remain behind bars until his trial, which was set for November.

Norvell's silence, his unremarkable past, and his ability to attack

Meredith despite the presence of law enforcement prompted widespread speculation. Many people shared a feeling of outrage: *How could officials have just stood by and done nothing to stop the shooting?* Others seemed annoyed: *Mississippi is getting blamed even though the shooter is from Tennessee!* Still others appeared bewildered: *Why hadn't Norvell—an experienced hunter with wartime commendation for marksmanship—used deadlier ammunition or aimed to kill?*

In the absence of a more logical narrative, people began to invent explanations for what had occurred. Maybe Norvell had acted on behalf of a white supremacy effort and the police were in on the plan, some speculated. Or maybe someone sympathetic to the civil rights movement had hired Norvell to shoot Meredith and make Mississippi look bad, others suggested. Those who avoided conspiracy theories were left to conclude that Norvell must have been a confused man during confusing times, acting alone for no apparent reason. Initial press coverage of the shooting compounded the chaos, for some of the earliest and most prominent reports mistakenly claimed that Meredith had been shot dead.

Local law enforcement officers apprehended Aubrey Norvell at the scene of Meredith's roadside shooting south of Hernando on June 6.

Martin Luther King, Jr., had followed the breaking news from his home base in Atlanta, Georgia, two states east of Mississippi. Even after it became clear that Meredith had survived, King and his allies in the civil rights movement prepared to respond. Words of sympathy and concern would not be enough, leaders agreed during phone calls and staff meetings. The movement's commitment to nonviolence required action, as well. Advocates for racial equality had to resume Meredith's effort—with or without him—and continue until they reached his objective of Jackson.

To do otherwise would allow violence to have the last word. Not acting would embolden those who opposed change.

Reaching that determination was easy; deciding how to execute the plan was not. The dimensions of the undertaking were staggering. Activists viewed the previous year's walk from Selma to Montgomery as an unprecedented achievement, but the logistical challenges of completing Meredith's hike dwarfed that undertaking by every measure. Distance. Time. Summer heat. Endless meals. Perpetual housing. Enormous costs. It would be a monumental challenge.

Movement leaders turned almost immediately to the Reverend James Lawson in Memphis for help. This veteran activist had joined the civil rights movement after meeting King in 1957. The two men shared a deep confidence in the power of nonviolence to bring about social change. Lawson had personally trained countless movement volunteers in the principles and practice of nonviolence, and many of his students had become essential activists in the struggle for equal rights. In 1962, Lawson had assumed leadership of Centenary United Methodist Church in Memphis, the region's largest congregation of black Methodists. His prominence in the movement, his leadership role in the local area, his experience with nonviolent protests, his organizational skills—all these factors and more made him an ideal ally in making plans for a renewed walk.

Movement leaders (from left) Floyd McKissick, Martin Luther King, Jr., and Stokely Carmichael converged on Meredith's hospital in Memphis, Tennessee, on June 7, one day after he'd been shot. Soon after the trio announced plans to revive his walk.

National leaders mobilized overnight, and by Tuesday, June 7, Lawson was welcoming them to Memphis. By day's end, leaders from all five of the nation's leading civil rights organizations—the so-called Big Five—would be in town. The first to arrive were

King, head of the Southern Christian Leadership Conference (SCLC) and Floyd McKissick, the newly appointed national director of the Congress of Racial Equality (CORE). They and some key associates piled into Lawson's family car and headed to the hospital to see Meredith.

Stokely Carmichael, the newly elected chairman of the Student Nonviolent Coordinating Committee (SNCC, pronounced "snick") arrived soon after, accompanied by additional representatives of his group. Leaders of two other organizations visited Meredith later that day, as well, Whitney Young of the National Urban League and Roy Wilkins of the National Association for the Advancement of Colored People (NAACP, spoken as "N-double-A-C-P").

Mississippi state troopers ordered marchers off the pavement when they began walking in honor of James Meredith on June 7. When King objected, an officer shoved him toward the roadside.

While Meredith, of course, knew all of the Big Five leaders by reputation, he found himself meeting some of them, such as King, for the first time. The arrival of such dignitaries at his bedside reinforced Meredith's sense of his own importance. King, McKissick, Lawson, and Carmichael offered Meredith their concern and presented him with a proposal. It was clear that he faced a lengthy recovery. He had dozens of open wounds that needed to heal, and he was in no condition to resume marching. While he recuperated, they asked, would he let them organize an effort to continue his walk? If he made a speedy recovery, he could rejoin them later on.

Overall the concept appealed to Meredith; he appreciated their endorsement of his effort and liked the idea of seeing it completed. But Meredith also realized that letting others carry on without him meant the walk would likely stray from his goals: Gone would be his plan for a small walk under his control from which he could exclude women and children. Meredith weighed the trade-offs and gave his visitors permission to proceed. The three leaders promised to seek his input while he recuperated and to keep Meredith updated as the walk progressed. Everyone agreed they needed to move fast.

Not even 24 hours had passed since Meredith's shooting, and the news was still hot. By acting quickly, organizers would receive vital media coverage that would boost the flow of volunteers and donations for their effort. Details would have to fall into place as they went. The first priority was to return to Highway 51. By doing so, the leaders would demonstrate the movement's determination to revive a campaign interrupted by violence. They made plans to start walking that very day from the spot where Meredith's blood had stained the highway. Before nightfall, more than a dozen men—including King, McKissick, Carmichael, and Lawson—had covered some six miles of new ground. Then they returned to their temporary base in Memphis to regroup.

That evening hundreds of people joined the day's marchers for a rally at Lawson's church. They sang freedom songs and listened to a parade of speakers. Representatives from each of the Big Five civil rights organizations shared their outrage over the shooting, their intention to complete the walk to Jackson, and their impatience with the pace of change. Wilkins, of the NAACP, spoke at the rally about how the residents of Meredith's home state seemed to be living in "another country" that followed a different set of laws and standards. He promised the crowd, "We are going to show the people of Mississippi that they are part of the 50 states," and therefore they must follow its laws. Speakers outlined the motivation for the effort, including their determination to answer a violent act with nonviolent solidarity.

But there were other reasons to act, as well. Like Meredith, they wanted to encourage blacks to become registered voters. And they hoped that their walk toward Jackson, when combined with shock over Meredith's shooting, would prompt members of Congress to pass the civil rights bill of 1966, the latest proposal in a series of such legislation. If approved, the bill would make it illegal to discriminate in housing and jury selection; extend federal protection to civil rights workers; and expand the integration of public schools. The march from Selma to Montgomery had influenced the passage of the Voting Rights Act of 1965; perhaps another great march—the Meredith march—would inspire lawmakers to act again.

Even as they fired up the local base and sent appeals for support to allies around the country, movement leaders still needed to determine how to pull off their plans. That night, after the public meeting at Lawson's church, representatives from the Big Five crammed into one of the guest rooms at the Lorraine Motel to establish the fundamentals. Slowly, over the course of a long and contentious discussion, civil rights leaders and their associates debated what to do.

Would voter registration be the focus of the march? Or passage of the civil rights bill? Both, if possible. They considered what roles whites should play in the protest. Some asked if whites should even be included at all: Wasn't it time for blacks to stand up on their own? Organizers compromised. Whites would be welcome to participate, but the effort would depend on African-American leadership and support.

Leaders debated the role of nonviolence versus the need for security. Could the Mississippi police be trusted to keep the marchers safe? Or should armed guards help protect participants? They finally agreed that the power of nonviolence would guide the effort; therefore, marchers would be unarmed. But, adopting a strategy already employed for other SNCC and CORE projects in the Deep South, members of a southern organization called the Deacons for Defense and Justice would accompany them as bodyguards, ready to defend the marchers from attacks by Klan members and other white supremacists.

Three of the Big Five groups had already expressed their support for a renewed march, and each brought its own strengths to the effort. McKissick's CORE could recruit plenty of volunteers but had little money. Carmichael's SNCC had the best sense of the territory they would cross, having done fieldwork in rural Mississippi since 1962. The SCLC, led by King, had access to donors. Furthermore, King's presence automatically guaranteed increased media coverage, funding, and participation. By joining forces, they might truly make a difference to the local people through voter registration drives while continuing the momentum of the national fight for civil rights. Maybe, as Carmichael hoped, their successes could "really make this the last march" for the movement.

The other Big Five leaders—Whitney Young of the National Urban League and Roy Wilkins of the NAACP—thought the goals for the revived walk were too fragmented. They wanted to focus only on passing the civil rights bill, not voter registration, too. And they regarded the militant tone of SNCC leaders as both counterproductive and offensive. Hearing the youthful Carmichael refer to Lyndon B. Johnson, the president of the United States, with street slang as "that cat Johnson," helped to send them packing. Their departure deprived the march of extra financial support and the appearance of Big Five unity, but it strengthened the ability of the participating trio of organizations to focus on their shared goals for the undertaking.

The remaining leaders crafted a document to summarize their motivations for the march, which they called their manifesto. This statement called on President Johnson to increase the nation's investment in the country's African-American citizens in four ways: enforcement of legal rights, increased economic opportunity, improved voting access, and greater representation by blacks on juries and police forces. Some of these concerns would be addressed by the proposed civil rights bill, but not all of them. Leaders of the revived march asked for broader action.

It was one o'clock in the morning by the conclusion of the meeting. Movement leaders settled down for a few hours of rest, knowing they'd be back on the road after daylight, traveling to the spot where they'd left off walking the day before. Until they could make more permanent arrangements, they planned to sleep in Memphis by night and walk in Mississippi by day, with each new hike extending their commute between the two locations.

Meredith remained in Memphis, too. Doctors had recommended he stay under observation at the hospital until he flew home to New York on Thursday. Those plans changed unexpectedly, though, on Wednesday, June 8. That morning, King and McKissick had stopped by Meredith's room to secure his support of their newly created manifesto. A hospital administrator interrupted their meeting to inform Meredith that he was to be discharged a day early. Regardless of his condition, hospital personnel had grown tired of the security concerns, news media attention, and high-profile visitors that accompanied his stay.

Meredith, King, and McKissick protested this unexpected eviction, but the hospital staff held firm. He had to leave that day. When Meredith tried to speak to reporters as he departed, he fainted from the sudden exertion and stress. Medical personnel revived him then ferried him to the curb in a wheelchair. Meredith flew home later that day. June Meredith had remained in New York with their six-year-old son, John, during her husband's walk and hospitalization. That evening she met his flight, joined by a throng of reporters. "I shall return to my divine responsibility," a weakened Meredith told the journalists, "and we shall reach our destination."

Despite his injuries—or, really, because of them—Meredith felt angry. He had entrusted his safety to local law enforcement officers, and they had failed him. Meredith, the military veteran who liked to plan with precision, wondered if he'd made a mistake when he'd brought a Bible to Mississippi instead of a gun. The day after his attack he had conveyed his frustration with dramatic language in a written statement for the press: "I could have knocked this intended killer off with one shot had I been prepared." Journalists knew the idea of anyone taking the law into his own hands, even in self-defense, could be seen as inflammatory and controversial. Thus, when reporters had the chance to question Meredith in New York, they pressed him on his comment and asked if he would arm himself should he be able to rejoin the campaign.

Meredith noted that he had turned to state officials for protection originally, and it hadn't worked; deputies had been present, but they had just stood by while Norvell took shots at him. Could he be confident they'd behave any differently the next time? Meredith told the reporters that if he could not count on receiving protection from local law enforcement personnel, then he had the right to consider arming himself in self-defense when he rejoined the march. When someone asked how he squared such a thought with the doctrine of nonviolence, Meredith replied, "Who the hell ever said I was nonviolent? I spent eight years in the military and the rest of my life in Mississippi."

Nonviolent protest or not, James Meredith didn't plan to get shot again.

"The shooting of James Meredith is further savage proof that brutality is still the white American way of life in Mississippi."

Floyd McKissick, national director for the Congress of Racial Equality (CORE), June 6, 1966

"Mississippi is emotionally and socially many miles from that point at which a person can work openly and honestly and even moderately for racial justice without some risk of verbal or physical attack."

Russell H. Barrett, professor at the University of Mississippi, speaking February 1, 1966

"Marching feet announce that time has come for a given idea. When the idea is a sound one, the cause a just one, and the demonstration a righteous one, change will be forthcoming. But if any of these conditions are not present, the power for change is missing also."

Martin Luther King, Jr., reflecting on the March Against Fear, October 1966

As marchers headed south through Mississippi on June 9, bystanders declared their support for segregation by waving the Confederate battle flag and performing the Confederacy's unofficial anthem, "Dixie."

CHAPTER 3

REVIVED

AMES MEREDITH'S WALK became important the minute James Meredith got shot. Before then, it had been a modest effort with only a few supporters. Aubrey Norvell changed that fact the moment he fired his shotgun at Meredith. But Meredith lost influence over his walk when he stopped participating in it, and he further faded in importance after he'd left the region. Even the title of his undertaking began to evolve in his absence.

Meredith had called his journey a Walk Against Fear. To him, a march equaled a protest. He hadn't seen his effort as a statement of protest; he'd just been trying to exercise his right to walk through his home state. But now Meredith's walk was becoming a protest. A protest against violence. A protest against racial fears. A protest in support of voter registration. A protest for further equality. As a consequence, Meredith's walk morphed into a march. The new venture went by many names. Organizers called it the Meredith Mississippi Freedom March in their manifesto. Some people shortened that name to the Meredith March. Others called it the Mississippi March. Over time it came to be known as the Meredith March Against Fear or, simply, the March Against Fear.

Whatever the endeavor's name, almost 200 miles separated organizers from Meredith's planned destination of Jackson. Tuesday's revival by civil rights leaders had been more symbolic than productive. The men had

DATES WALKED: June 8–11 **MILES WALKED:** 37 **ROUTE:** North of Coldwater to north of Pope

covered just six miles. It would take many days of dedicated hiking to complete the journey, many days and countless volunteers.

By Wednesday, June 8, those volunteers began to materialize. When Martin Luther King, Jr., and others returned to the day's starting point, they were heartened to find a gathering of hikers on hand to join them. The group numbered about 120 as it headed south on Highway 51 toward the nearby town of Coldwater and beyond. Most of the day's walkers were African Americans. Some were local residents; others had traveled by chartered bus from Memphis, inspired by the previous night's rally there.

Few of these participants planned to hike for long, and that was okay. Organizers viewed their endeavor as more of a relay than a marathon. It didn't matter whether someone walked for days on end or for just a few hours. What mattered was for some group of people to keep walking, over time, until they reached Jackson. Thus the composition of the march evolved day by day, as people hugged the side of the road and trudged south under the summer sun. Sometimes movement leaders marched out front—leading—but on other occasions they mingled with the crowd. While they walked, participants often sang freedom songs or chanted the words "freedom" and its Swahili equivalent, "Uhuru," showing solidarity with blacks involved in the struggle for racial equality in Africa.

Even though Wednesday's group had gotten a late start, by 5 p.m. hikers had covered more than six miles and reached the outskirts of the next town, Senatobia. Then everyone dispersed for the night. Some headed to their local residences, but most returned, yet again, to Memphis, where they slept in homes, motel rooms, and even on the floor of James Lawson's church, which had become the temporary headquarters for the march.

Hosea Williams of the SCLC coordinated an army of volunteers from this makeshift base of operations. His team handled everything from recruitment and meal planning to housing and drafting news bulletins for the media. Organizers raced to arrange the logistics that would eliminate the need for commuting to and from the march site. Not only would it become increasingly impractical as volunteers hiked farther and farther away from Memphis, but it undercut the momentum of the effort.

Participants in the previous year's march from Selma to Montgomery had camped along the way and shared evening rallies that built camaraderie. Leaders wanted to create that same atmosphere again. Plus they hoped the march through Mississippi would grow in popularity over time, swelling to a crescendo of thousands by its conclusion. The best way to build a sense of unity, to build a bigger crowd, was to add momentum—and people—day by day as they marched toward Jackson. That meant renting tents, finding camping sites, arranging for sanitation facilities, setting daily hiking goals, scouting out picnic spots for lunch breaks, and finding volunteers who could feed marchers and help with transportation.

All the while, as organizers organized, marchers kept walking south, mile by mile.

Thursday, June 9, saw a delayed start, too, but, even so, marchers covered nine miles before stopping at 4 p.m. just beyond the town of Como. More than 200 people had turned out for the hike, including a local man named Armistead Phipps who insisted that he had to take part in the event regardless of his heart condition. "This is the greatest thing that has ever happened to our people in Mississippi," Phipps declared. "Now they won't be afraid to vote anymore."

That morning the 58-year-old man had headed for the starting point near Senatobia and waited patiently for King's arrival from Memphis. But after walking for a short while, Phipps stumbled and collapsed. Despite medical attention, he died soon after. His passing was both distressing and problematic. The pool of news reporters that was shadowing the revived hike often swelled to a hundred or more, and any of them could have blamed this fatality on the march, creating coverage that undercut the entire endeavor. King deflected criticism from the march to Mississippi itself by connecting the Phipps death to the trials of living under segregation in the state. "His death means that he was probably underfed, overworked and underpaid," King observed. Phipps hadn't died because he'd walked for freedom; he had died because of his lack of freedom during his lifetime as a black man in the Deep South.

King had a point.

Mississippi ranked as the poorest state in the nation in 1966, and racism contributed extensively to that status. The impoverishment of the state was almost inevitable given that nearly half its residents were African American and that whites had constructed a segregated society that worked to disadvantage them. The vast majority of the state's black residents were descendants of slaves who had been freed with no assets into a post–Civil War world that offered few opportunities. Poverty became one's inheritance, passed down, generation by generation, as an invisible chain of bondage. The places that many of them called home looked like shacks, not houses. Cardboard and tarpaper often filled in for siding. Few houses had indoor plumbing. Generation after generation of African Americans tried to turn nothing into something, but that's hard to do when one's world is rigged to give the advantage to people with white skin.

An older woman watched through her screen door as marchers passed her rural Mississippi home. Undated photo.

When the federal government tried to intervene on behalf of blacks, local whites resisted. After the U.S. Supreme Court ordered the integration of public schools in 1954, Mississippi legislators considered abolishing their public schools. In the end, they continued the state's education system but provided publicly funded vouchers to help white families send their children to segregated private schools. When the federal government offered vital food supplies and provided free services such as health care and preschool education to Mississippi's poor, many whites criticized the programs as an alarming imposition of federal will on one of its 50 states. Such criticism was hypocritical because many whites benefited from federal aid, too. But, whites tended to view their own government support, such as a generous crop subsidy program for cotton farmers, as valid even as they dismissed federal handouts for poor people, who were so often black.

The few whites who expressed their disagreement with segregationists risked condemnation, loss of business support, and more. Even when only a minority of whites in a community joined supremacist organizations such as the Ku Klux Klan and local White Citizens' Councils, their voices and actions came, by default, to represent the white majority.

As a result, it took outsiders and mass action to break down a system nurtured by centuries of slavery and 100 years of post–Civil War segregation. Mississippi had become so segregated that whites might not even realize the depths of its racial oppression. They saw blacks on their terms—as maids, as field hands, as customers. Whites were far more likely to attribute the lag in the advancement of such folks to some inherent lack of ability or to an innate dislike of hard work rather than acknowledge the yoke of impoverishment and hopelessness that was the legacy of slavery.

Civil rights leaders wanted to peel back the veneer that made segregation seem okay. They'd made progress in Alabama. They'd made progress in other states in the South. But civil rights leaders had found Mississippi to be tough territory in the past, and no one could be sure that this time would be different.

Still, they marched.

On Friday, June 10, the fourth day of the revived march, 155 people set off on a 15-mile route, heading toward Sardis and points beyond. Locals welcomed the marchers to their town with a homemade picnic lunch; then some 100 residents from the area joined hikers for the day's remaining 10 miles. Even more people joined the procession as it neared its stopping point in Batesville, allowing the day's march to conclude with a crowd of more than 500 participants. Local blacks once again fed the marchers, offering up a feast that included barbecue, fried chicken, fresh vegetables, corn bread, and desserts.

Perhaps best of all, the first tent had arrived. Three more would follow in the coming days. For the first time, hikers had the option to sleep along the route. No more commuting. Volunteers erected the rented circus tent on the grounds of a local church, and some 300 people bedded down for the night, intent on resuming their hike the next morning.

By sleeping on-site, the marchers were able to make an earlier departure than on previous days. On Saturday morning, June 11, hundreds of them paraded into Batesville bound for their first stop at a county courthouse. The courthouses of Mississippi served as the hubs for voter registration in the state, and the Panola County courthouse offered organizers a prime spot to test their influence on voter registration. Some marchers literally danced into town, singing freedom songs, clapping, and swaying in time to an irresistible beat. *Courage, freedom, justice,* the rhythm seemed to say. *Have courage. Seek freedom. Find justice.* Many African Americans found the call impossible to ignore.

"When I saw them marching, I decided I wanted my freedom," explained one black man who'd come to town intending to do errands but who ended up with a voter registration card. Others lined up likewise to enter the building and emerge as registered voters. Marchers cheered and hoisted aloft a 100-plus-year-old man whose age practically assured he had been born into slavery. Now he had lived long enough to register to vote.

Few local whites would have supported such moments, but for the majority who disapproved of the activism it seemed better to tolerate it than to resist, especially with national news reporters on hand to document any confrontations. Better to speed things along and hope the procession would soon move on down the road. By midday, marchers were indeed again under way. Seven miles later they reached a campsite near Pope.

At week's end, organizers and volunteers could feel the growing momentum. They'd covered almost 40 miles since Wednesday. Locals were joining the march. Folks were lining up to register to vote. More tents were on order.

And Jackson got closer every day.

"If you and enough of your fellow Americans answer this call, perhaps we may yet see a day when the marching can stop, when any man walking in this land does so solely for his pleasure, when it would never occur to him that by doing so he risks his life."

Appeal from the organizers of the March Against Fear, seeking participants in their revival of James Meredith's attempt to walk through Mississippi

"To expect a group of people raised and nurtured for 100 years on a system they evidently didn't think was wrong and expect them to agree that the whole thing has been wrong and to reverse themselves and change at once . . . that's asking too much of human nature."

A white planter near Greenwood, Mississippi, commenting in 1964 on the challenges whites faced in trying to keep pace with changing times

"There are things we used to do
that we don't know why we did them.
We didn't know why we did them **then."**

Joseph Lee, editor of the *Daily Sentinel-Star* newspaper, Grenada, Mississippi

A group of African-American students from the University of Mississippi marched in a show of solidarity with James Meredith. They often wore clothing emblazoned with the Ole Miss name and logo. Undated photo.

CHAPTER 4

DELTA BOUND

ITH MOMENTUM BUILDING five days into the revived march, movement leaders decided at their customary end-of-day planning meeting on Saturday, June 11, to change course after a few more days of walking. Instead of maintaining James Meredith's due-south route all the way to Jackson, they would veer away from Highway 51 when the group reached Grenada and detour west into the flat, open countryside of the Mississippi Delta.

Meredith's route had suited his own purposes quite nicely. It was direct. It passed not far from his birthplace of Kosciusko. It was familiar, serving as his preferred route when driving through the state. But Meredith's route didn't necessarily serve the goals of the revived walk. His course bypassed the delta, a region densely populated by African Americans. In some areas, blacks outnumbered whites there by two to one, or more. If the newly constituted March Against Fear really wanted to register a lot of black voters, then it made sense to take the campaign to the places where they lived.

True, they'd have farther to walk, about 50 miles farther, in fact. The new route would curve west toward the Mississippi River, drop south, then bend back toward the center of the state, rejoining Highway 51 near the city of Canton. The diversion would take longer, a week longer, they figured. And certainly the effort would grow more costly and complicated.

DATES WALKED: June 12–13 **MILES WALKED:** 33 **ROUTE:** North of Pope to north of Grenada

Those were the downsides. But the upsides made the change seem worth it. Perhaps the best advantage of all was that their new course would take marchers directly through areas where Stokely Carmichael and his SNCC associates had worked for years. They knew these people. They had contacts there.

These folks were primed for change.

The new route traversed territory thick with racial tensions. The delta had been cotton-growing country since the era of slavery. In fact, slaves and their descendants had fueled the region's wealth even as those who toiled the hardest remained the area's poorest residents. Since the early 20th century, thousands of African Americans had fled the delta and moved north or west. They grew tired of the trap of sharecropping, where landowners controlled all the cash flow and few dollars made it back to laborers who tended endless rows of cotton. They grew tired of the racial attitudes that undercut any sense of self-worth—being called "boy" for life, being expected to step off sidewalks when whites approached, being excluded from services whites reserved for themselves—an endless string of humiliations. And, perhaps most of all, they grew tired of living their lives in fear, afraid of persecution by white individuals or by the almost uniformly all-white criminal justice system.

Blacks who escaped to cities beyond the South continued to face racial bias, but they left the harshest edges of their old lives behind. Those who remained in the South had to navigate the southern world order and its carefully constructed code of racial behaviors and beliefs. This rule by segregation had evolved from attitudes that flourished during the time of slavery, when whites used any means of terror or force necessary to control the people they owned. A hundred years after slavery, one's race still influenced every interaction, whether folks thought about it or not, because skin color was the defining trait for navigating the region's laws, customs, and privileges.

That layer of distance made it easier for southern whites to define African Americans as outsiders, as others. When people are viewed as others, they stop being seen as fellow human beings and are judged by their differences instead of their commonalities. Those differences can become threatening, can become something to be afraid of, something to oppress. Othering breeds a curious loop of fear. One group becomes afraid of another and asserts its superiority by instilling terror in the second group. The fear caused by this terror is so gripping that it's easy to overlook the fear that motivates the attackers. Yet southern whites were full of fears about the people they oppressed.

Whites feared they would lose their subservient labor force. Or that they would lose their own jobs if blacks had equal access to work. Or that they would end up having to take orders from blacks. They feared that blacks would advance ahead of whites up the social ladder. Or that African Americans would take revenge on them for past mistreatments. Or that black activists were somehow tied to Soviet-style communism. They feared that if they, as whites, spoke out against segregation, they could be shunned or attacked by other whites. So segregation persisted, as did the cycle of fear it fed among people of any color.

A Mississippi news story from Sunday, June 12, illustrated the relentless cycle of fear and violence. That day, the body of Ben Chester White turned up in Pretty Creek, an unassuming stream in the southwestern corner of the state. White was an African American in his mid-60s who had suffered a gruesome death. Bullets riddled his body; a close-range shotgun blast had nearly severed his head from his torso. Later on it would come out that he'd been murdered two days before by three local white men. They'd coaxed White into their car on the pretext of looking for a lost dog. Then they'd murdered him. "Oh, Lord, what have I done to deserve this?" White reportedly asked just before his death.

White's murderers hoped the dead man would become a decoy who would draw Martin Luther King, Jr., into their community, just as Meredith's shooting had brought the civil rights icon to Mississippi. After King appeared, they planned to murder him, too. King, however, rather than being diverted to attend to this new tragedy, remained focused on the march toward Jackson. The same day White's body emerged from Pretty Creek, he celebrated the life of Armistead Phipps, the man who had collapsed during the march three days before. Phipps had died with a poll tax receipt in his pocket, showing that he had previously registered to vote and had paid the fee that entitled him to cast his ballot. Such taxes had served for decades as one more way to discourage voter participation by impoverished minorities. Yet Phipps had found the funds required and the courage it took to pay them. "This was a man who was not afraid," King preached at Phipps's funeral.

While King spoke, marchers continued their trek down Highway 51 toward Grenada. Now that organizers had tents, they began perfecting their system for hiking and camping. In order to cover as many miles as possible each day, they permitted the heartiest hikers to push on even when other walkers were ready to stop. When necessary, camp supply trucks and other vehicles traveled back up the highway to fetch participants who fell short of the evening's destination or headed beyond the campsite to collect walkers who had progressed even farther. The point where one day's hike ended became the spot where walking resumed the next morning, with vehicles once again transporting walkers, as needed. This relay of marchers was a creative way to cover significant amounts of ground each day without requiring constant participation by everyone. No one expected all the marchers to cover every mile. What mattered was for some combination of them to walk every mile.

The availability of transport created flexibility in other ways, too. Sometimes organizers pulled up stakes and moved the group's campsite every day, but on other occasions they gained permission to stay a second night at a location, as was the case on Sunday, June 12, when the group erected its tents near Enid Dam, south of Pope, Mississippi. Sleeping twice in one spot eliminated the hassle of breaking camp daily. Hikers could just keep going, as they did that day to cover a record-setting 19 miles on foot before riding back to their base. Despite heavy showers, the sturdiest walkers covered 14 additional miles the next day before they returned for a second night at Enid Dam.

Some people marched day after day. Many could volunteer for only a brief time before having to return to their jobs and other responsibilities. Some folks hiked for miles at a time. Others participated for short distances, such as when the procession passed near their homes. Many walkers came from Mississippi or nearby Memphis, but at various times representatives from nearly every state in the Union took part in the march.

Walkers arrived at their third campsite (viewed from the earthen summit of Enid Dam) on June 12.

African Americans outnumbered whites overall, but a small group of white volunteers joined the black and white representatives of the sponsoring organizations to form an essential core of persistent marchers while countless other hikers came and went.

The march was too impromptu for a roster of participants to have been kept, and so it is impossible to size up the endeavor with detailed statistics, but the historical record holds clues about its diversity. Blacks and whites, everyone from northern ministers to members of a Chicago street gang. A group of African-American students who had followed James Meredith to Ole Miss. People in their 70s and families with young children. Executives and waiters. College students and couples on their honeymoons. Traditional folks in Sunday-pressed clothes and counterculture hippies with scruffy hair and guitars. A state patrol officer pronounced the procession to be "a great assembly of kooks."

Participants experienced a richness of diversity that would have been almost impossible to find in their individual lives. Blacks and whites talked together, walked together, shared camp chores together, and slept in the same tents, separated by gender. And they walked as equals with the luminaries of the civil rights movement. Any given day might find King, Carmichael, and Floyd McKissick marching alongside them, or Andrew Young and Hosea Williams from King's SCLC. Or Willie Ricks and Cleveland Sellers from Carmichael's SNCC. McKissick, whose family even marched with the group for a time, often set the pace on days with many miles to cover. James Lawson made regular commutes from his Memphis church to march. The state's black leaders for equality turned out, too. Noted local activist Fannie Lou Hamer, for example, added not just her courageous spirit but her powerful singing to many miles of hiking.

Almost every night, march leaders and participants gathered together—outdoors if they were camping in the countryside or, when staying in a town, at a welcoming church. These evening meetings reinforced the sense of community among the marchers. The programs included everything from announcements to the singing of freedom songs to prayers. And then there were the speeches. Not all leaders were present every night. Sometimes they had to leave the march because of business meetings or to honor prior commitments. King and the SCLC had an extended outreach project in Chicago, for example, that he needed to monitor. King left to raise money for the march, too, speaking in northern communities that were more sympathetic to the cause of civil rights. But whoever was on-site filled the evening program with stirring rhetoric, testimonials about surviving hardship, and encouragement that better times were coming.

Each day marchers were tested by the everyday whims of their environment. Skies filled with fluffy clouds, and skies blanketed in threatening grays. Breezes one day. Heavy stillness the next. Ever present heat most days. Cloudbursts on others. Air that dripped with humidity. Symphonies of frogs calling from swampy bayous. The humming of insects along endless roadways. Sunrises that promised a new day. Evenings dotted with stars.

Even as participants marched against fear, they faced it constantly. In the hateful looks of passing white motorists. In the potential threat those

Fannie Lou Hamer spoke at campsite rallies as a veteran of the fight for racial equality in Mississippi. Undated photo.

vehicles posed as they whizzed past. In the shadows of the roadside underbrush that could easily have harbored more shooters like Aubrey Norvell. In the sounds that came with darkness as marchers stretched out on uneven ground underneath their tents, trying to sleep through muggy nights. In the unsettling splashes of the red, white, and blue of the Confederate battle flag.

Everyone knew they walked with danger. Volunteers from afar who passed through the organizational hub in Memphis were reminded of that fact when they registered to march. Beyond the usual questions of name and home address, the registration form asked marchers to identify their blood type, physical description, scars, other defining marks, medical history, and next of kin. Organizers would need to know whom to contact in case someone became ill, or injured, or worse. Accompanying instructions urged marchers to leave Mississippi immediately after they'd finished their contribution to the protest, whether they walked for a few days or for weeks.

The daily hikes unfolded with an illusion of safety since the marchers traveled with considerable law enforcement representation. *But, then, so had Meredith*, they may have thought, *and what good had that done?* Dozens of state troopers and county deputies accompanied them. *But weren't these the same white men who normally harassed local blacks?* Members of the FBI shadowed the process. *But were these agents there to protect participants or to spy on them?* "The state provided some protection," Lawson wrote later that summer. "But we were always in doubt as to whether it was protection for us against violence or protection for segregation against us."

In the absence of confidence in formal law enforcement officials, armed members of the Deacons for Defense and Justice continued to accompany the march. This outfit had formed in Louisiana during 1964 in response to the violence and tensions that developed in the South over the advance of civil rights. Most of their work during the march through Mississippi took place at night, which allowed the walk itself to be a demonstration of the power of nonviolence. Members of the group guarded campsites, listened in on two-way radios to make sure no Klansmen were nearby, and escorted convoys of marchers and dignitaries when they left the oversight of local and state law enforcement officials. The presence of armed guards irritated some of the hardiest advocates of nonviolence, but plenty of participants welcomed their company.

Music had always provided an essential soundtrack to the civil rights movement, and it continued to do so. Marchers sang freedom songs. They sang spirituals. They sang songs of protest. Singing built bonds between strangers. It bonded people in a way that not only made them sing in unison, but made them feel in unison. This resulting strength-of-the-sum-being-greater-than-its-individual-parts served as the backbone of nonviolent protest, both because it built camaraderie and because it instilled the singers with courage. Instead of being afraid, marchers sang. It helped.

Although safety was an overarching concern, so were the everyday logistics required to support a roving band of activists hiking through rural countryside in summer heat. "It's typical 'Freedom Movement' organization," observed one veteran of past protests. "No one knows what's going on, yet everything manages to get done." In an era long before the development of disposable plastic water bottles, trucks hauled drinking water to strategic positions for distribution. A community medical organization provided mobile first aid. Meals happened with predictable frequency, but menus varied from odd (hot dogs for breakfast), to frugal (bologna and crackers), to surprising (fresh peaches instead of canned ones), to awkward

Few hikers carried provisions while they walked, so rest breaks for food and drink became essential during the long, hot days of the march. Undated photo.

(a meal served with knives as the only available eating utensil). And then there were the feasts. Over and over, local women prepared family-reunion-worthy meals for the marchers. Fried chicken, ham sandwiches, and apple pie. Barbecue, and fresh beans, and cakes. Marchers may have faced fears, but they rarely faced hunger.

Local African Americans supported the march in other ways, too, opening their homes, sharing bedding for campsites, publicizing related events, and joining in the endeavor themselves. It took considerable courage to register during the march's voting drives. Each person had to weigh his or her individual circumstances: *Might I lose my job if I register to vote? Might a family member lose a job? Might local whites refuse to do business with me? Might I or someone in my family be threatened or attacked? Are times really changing? What's going to happen after all these brave folks leave town? Will I be sorry then that I stuck out my neck and joined in? Will I be sorry if I don't?* As one elderly local man put it during the extended campaign: "When you have a custom of being afraid since you're a baby, it's hard to shake." He chose not to register when the march passed through his town.

Blacks in Mississippi had faced so many obstacles to voting for so long that it could easily have seemed hard to believe times really were changing. Except for the brief federally enforced Reconstruction era right after the Civil War, the attitudes that had prevailed before that war still held sway. Voting had always been the privilege of white people, and they seemed intent on keeping it that way. To many of Mississippi's black citizens, whites were just in charge. Always had been. Seemingly always would be. Thus, even after the passage of the Voting Rights Act of 1965, few African Americans had registered to vote in Mississippi.

In 1964, one year before its passage, about 70 percent of whites who were old enough to vote had registered. Not even 7 percent of blacks had done so. Two years later, at the time of the March Against Fear, that figure had climbed to just over 22 percent. But that still left nearly half a million eligible African Americans who had not registered to vote. Even in counties where blacks outnumbered whites, it was rare for whites not to represent the majority of registered voters. When blacks did begin to register and vote in 1965, state and local governments began passing laws that diminished the impact of black voters, such as redrawing statewide voting districts to the advantage of white residents and removing neighborhood representation from local elections. Such efforts intensified during the 1966 march through the state.

A surprising number of African Americans lived such isolated lives in Mississippi, and had grown up with such limited access to schooling, that they had no idea of their rights—or even that voting existed. For those who did, just the mechanics of the process might seem intimidating. How to register. How to mark a ballot. The concept of secret ballots. The particulars of the election process, including its primaries, local elections, and national ones. Even the schedule of voting could be confusing. Some of the poorest potential voters had never learned to read, creating yet another barrier to the process. All this unfamiliarity bred one more layer of anxiety. Never mind being afraid of how some white person might react to a black voter.

Just figuring out how to vote could be scary.

“I think the daylight’s breakin’.”

P. L. Elion, age 87, a Mississippi resident and son of a slave, after witnessing the March Against Fear

“If we remain segregationists at heart, we never need abandon our hope of restoring our Southern way of life.”

Newspaper editorial denouncing the March Against Fear, from the *Meridian Star*, Meridian, Mississippi

of America . . . The white man is in dire need of the Negro to free him of his guilt, and the Negro is in dire need of the white man to free him of his fear."

Martin Luther King, Jr., speaking to participants in the March Against Fear, June 12, 1966

Marchers and local residents gathered for a voter registration rally on the courthouse square in Grenada on June 14. A monument honoring the Confederacy towered over the crowd.

CHAPTER 5

BLACK POWER

N TUESDAY, JUNE 14, the core group of marchers left their Enid Dam campsite for the last time, rode in trucks to the place where they'd stopped hiking the day before, and walked the remaining nine miles to Grenada, Mississippi, the group's turning point away from Highway 51. This sizable city served as a county seat, so participants planned to conduct a voter registration drive there before heading west on state roads toward delta country.

Until the arrival of the March Against Fear, no one from the civil rights movement had ever done outreach in Grenada. Community leaders decided to adopt the same strategy that Batesville's had employed. Avoid confrontation, appear accommodating, hope the procession doesn't linger long. In short: Put up with it. Meanwhile, local blacks found the enthusiasm of the passing throng irresistible. "COME ON OVER, BROTHER, COME ON OVER, BROTHER," chanted the corps of 200 marchers as it wound its way through the segregated neighborhoods of Grenada. "I was just looking," one woman admitted to a news reporter, "and all of a sudden I was marching." The throng doubled in size and then expanded again until 500 people were converging on the city's town square.

Just as travelers could count on finding a courthouse at the heart of every county seat, anyone who visited just about any southern town—county seat

DATES WALKED: June 14–16 **MILES WALKED:** Almost 42 **ROUTE:** North of Grenada to north of Greenwood

or otherwise—could expect to find a memorial to the Confederate cause in the city center. These landmarks didn't just commemorate a period that had divided the nation a century earlier; they commemorated a way of life that divided it still. African Americans would have seen little to celebrate in monuments to a campaign that sought to keep their ancestors enslaved, but whites saw them differently.

When Robert Green, a march organizer, climbed onto the base of Grenada's memorial to the Civil War, local whites didn't see a psychology professor from Michigan State University. Nor did they see a valuable member of the SCLC leadership team. They saw a black man climbing a revered memorial to the Confederacy, and they didn't like it one bit. "We're tired of seeing rebel flags," Green said from his perch on the monument. "Give me the flag of the United States, the flag of freedom!" Local whites gasped as he removed a Confederate battle flag that had been lodged behind the sculpted face of Confederate president Jefferson Davis. March participants and local blacks cheered as the American flag took its place. "We want Brother Jefferson Davis to know that the South he represented will never rise again," Green told the crowd. "This is not the Confederacy, this is America!"

Green's language and behavior challenged everything Grenada's memorial and innumerable others throughout the South had come to represent. Such monuments reinforced a twisted interpretation of the historical record that portrayed the Confederate side of the conflict in noble and flattering terms. Proponents called their account the Lost Cause, and its fiction had morphed into accepted fact in the South and beyond, through generations of countless repetitions within families and schools.

The Lost Cause story relieved whites of the guilt they might otherwise have felt about past ties to slavery and rebellion. It spun tales of slaves and masters living in harmony and caring about each other, almost as if they were family members. It minimized the injustices of slavery, the way that slave owners divided husband from wife and parent from child, the system of terror and cruelty that drove slaves in their forced labor, the sexual exploitation of enslaved women by their masters.

This narrative maintained that slavery hadn't even been the basis for the Civil War. Rather than fighting for the right to own slaves, the South had fought for the right of states to disagree with the federal government. As for the war itself, the Lost Cause storyline promoted the noble purpose of Confederate soldiers who had fought valiantly to defend their homelands against invasion. It presented Union generals as cruel conquerors and portrayed postwar Reconstruction as a corrupt occupation by northern carpetbaggers. The Lost Cause proclaimed the inferiority of former slaves and asserted their need for continued supervision under the leadership and controlling care of ruling whites. This fiction led to the systematic segregation of the races and the oppression of African Americans into modern times.

Robert Green addressed his comments on June 14 to the crowd and to Jefferson Davis, the historical figure commemorated on Grenada's Civil War memorial.

The shock value of Green's actions in Grenada was ensured by the context of the Lost Cause story. It's not surprising that local whites gasped at his boldness, but the presence of national news media discouraged them from retaliating. "All we want is to get these people through town and out of here," said Grenada's city manager. And so white officials registered new voters and hired extra registrars from the African-American community to help with the increased demand. Bowing to pressure from the activists, they converted previously segregated bathrooms into integrated facilities.

The fears of many of the city's black residents

Racist graffiti greeted marchers on the day they visited Grenada, June 14.

dissolved amid such empowering evidence of change. "All of a sudden, out of nowhere," one teen said, he'd felt "injected with a sense of courage, defiance, outspokenness." He was too young to register, but nearly 200 other black residents of Grenada did so. Combined with another push for registration in town the next day, a total of 814 people became eligible to participate in coming elections, more than double the previous registration of African Americans in the area.

But the white establishment wasn't going to give up without a fight. After the marchers departed, local officials restored the segregated signs to the courthouse bathroom doors, fired the black registrars, and began to harass the few organizers who had remained for further activism. Staff members from the U.S. Department of Justice had started shadowing the march after James Meredith's shooting to make sure state officials were complying with federal laws. Some of these staffers, including assistant attorney general John Doorr, lingered in Grenada so they could document and address the local defiance of national laws. The march was leaving a messy legacy in its wake.

Paul Johnson, Mississippi's governor, began to question his state's strategy of accommodating the activists. Johnson had gained fame when he was lieutenant governor in 1962 during the standoff over Meredith's enrollment in Ole Miss. As governor, he had decided initially to protect participants in the revived march; he didn't want any more shootings or bad publicity. But this wasn't an ordinary protest march; it had "turned into a voter registration campaign," he said, and he saw no need to continue to provide an abundance of protection for the marchers. "We are not going to be in the position of wet-nursing a group of showmen," he declared.

Sometimes participants carried flags and homemade signs when they marched through communities. Locals often joined the procession of marchers, walking together for a common cause. Undated photo.

The governor reduced the march's security detail from 20 state patrol squad cars to 4. As for Mississippi's Confederate monuments, state officials ordered six African Americans—men who were serving time at Parchman, the state penitentiary—to protect them. From then on, law enforcement officials transported prison inmates from site to site along the march route to serve as guards for the memorials. This assignment forced the men to protect monuments that honored the very soldiers who had fought to keep their ancestors enslaved.

On Wednesday, June 15, participants left the pavement of U.S. Highway 51 and headed west. Some 140 miles of delta flatlands lay ahead on rural roads that wound past swamps, cotton fields, scrubby forests, and poverty on their route back toward Highway 51. This territory held towns so small that marchers could easily outnumber the inhabitants. That first night, after hiking

15 miles, the procession reached the hamlet of Holcomb, population 97 at the time of the 1960 census. A few dozen marchers walked another two miles just to give the group a head start the next day.

By this point, organizers for the march had added a divide-and-conquer strategy in order to expand the influence of their outreach even further. Mississippi had 82 counties, and, even by sweeping through the delta, marchers would only pass through 10 of them. So the activists put together satellite expeditions to encourage voter registration in six additional counties. Crowds formed whenever the legendary Martin Luther King, Jr., appeared, whether he was on the main route or traveled to one of the new stops beyond it. Just seeing King, let alone hearing him speak, could empower action.

"It was like the messiah walking through the community," recalled one SNCC organizer on a visit to Indianola in rural Sunflower County. A five-year-old girl who heard King speak in Cleveland, Mississippi, dissolved into tears over the power of his appeals. "I want to go with him," she sobbed repeatedly. But fear dogged these efforts, too. "Get out of here, nigger, and get out fast," ordered a white man when a SNCC worker stopped to distribute information at a local eatery in Charleston, Mississippi. Before the activist could retreat, he was punched in the face.

Such incidents found their way into the daily media reports on television and in newspapers around the country. Among those following the reports was the man who had inspired the protest in the first place: James Meredith. Meredith recognized that a distance of more than miles was growing between him and the endeavor that was taking place in his honor. Nine days after his shooting, and a week after leaving Memphis, he reasserted his relevance to the march by holding a press conference in New York State.

"There seems to be a good bit of show going on down there," observed Meredith, his feisty spirit clearly intact. The revived march "is not a testing ground for the various organizations to test the popularity and strength of their leaders," he declared. It's a campaign to "gain respect for the Negro." Meredith, referencing his years in the military, suggested that the effort seemed to lack a clear chain of command. He disapproved of the involvement of women in the march. He wasn't wild about the plan to veer away from Highway 51. In short, he didn't see enough of himself in the new march, and he planned to change that. As soon as doctors said he was ready, he'd be back, maybe as early as the beginning of the next week.

Fan mail—and hate mail—poured into the Meredith household during his recuperation. Telegrams, cards, and letters. From friends, from family, from the governor of New York State, from strangers. "You say you don't believe in nonviolence," wrote one angry white citizen. "Well if you believe in violence, why don't we have a civil war to decide which is the more powerful race? I don't think it will be a contest. I think the white people would win. So anytime you want this, we will be ready." The writer signed the note with initials only.

Most correspondents were more sympathetic. Some enclosed small amounts of money with their notes to help with Meredith's medical bills or to support his drive for voter registration. A few penned poems in his honor. One woman ordered a tree to be planted in his name in Israel. Another wrote to say she was "ashamed to belong to a race who believes itself superior." Children carefully printed out words of sympathy and advice: "My classmates all said hello and hope your back gets well," wrote a young girl from a New York City public school. "I hope you help people to not make violence," urged a male classmate. Another boy advised him, "Next time make sure you have a gun on you," seeming to share Meredith's concern that he might not be able to depend on law enforcement officers for his protection.

On Thursday, June 16, hikers carried on from their endpoint on the previous day and made steady progress toward their next destination, Greenwood, the Leflore County seat. For SNCC coordinator Stokely Carmichael, reaching Greenwood meant a homecoming. Carmichael had joined protests in Mississippi as far back as 1961, when, as a student at Howard University, he'd taken part in the Freedom Rides for integrated interstate transportation. He'd refused bail alongside fellow protesters and turned 20 at Parchman Penitentiary. During his incarceration, he had participated in further nonviolent protests, including a hunger strike, alongside other activists. Carmichael had returned to Mississippi the following two summers to help in Greenwood on SNCC projects, and he'd begun working there full time on voter registration drives and other SNCC initiatives after his graduation.

Carmichael had formed strong bonds with Greenwood residents, and everyone seemed to know him, including local law enforcement personnel who had jailed him for his activism on multiple occasions. The young organizer had infused his outreach there with tireless enthusiasm, incredible courage, and considerable charm. Local blacks loved him. Local whites, not so much. To them, he was one of those so-called outside agitators who had begun to invade the South, stirring people up and putting unwelcome ideas into their heads. Lanky and tall, at just over six feet, he liked to show up at meetings in overalls. Nothing fancy, just looking like everyday folks. He had a keen intelligence and a willingness to speak his mind. Friends nicknamed him Stokely Starmichael because of his ability to befriend and inspire local blacks. Allies called him the Delta Devil because of his talents at high-speed driving—a handy skill when it came time to outrun cars in hot pursuit, whether driven by hostile cops or hostile Klansmen.

Despite the persistent efforts of Carmichael and other SNCC workers, Greenwood remained stubbornly segregated. Only about a third of its citizens were white, but this white minority dominated the majority population of blacks. Although it was among the state's larger municipalities, a mere 250 African Americans there had managed to navigate the obstacles of fear, fraud, and intimidation that kept so many blacks off the voter registries.

Even before the marchers reached Greenwood, whites in the area expressed their dislike that Carmichael was returning in the company of a protest march. Cars buzzed past the hikers with such threatening intensity that Robert Green ordered participants to sit down and hold their ground. "We've had enough of that!" he declared. "I want this stopped." He refused to proceed until officers from their diminished highway patrol intervened. Greenwood city officials, apprehensive about the approaching throng, put the city's entire police force on alert with rotating rounds of duty, day and night. The mayor began begging the governor to send more state troopers to defend his town from what he saw as impending invasion.

March organizers intended to camp in Greenwood beside the city's segregated elementary school, pursuing a policy of asserting their right to make use of public land. On the appointed day, though, local officials refused to accommodate their plan. Word of the housing snafu reached Carmichael as he hiked, and he left the procession to travel ahead of the marchers and confront the problem.

In an era before cellular phones, public phone booths provided an essential communications link for marchers and organizers. Stokely Carmichael emerged from one playfully marked with the SNCC acronym. Undated photo.

Carmichael reached Greenwood in a fighting mood. After police officials forbade him to erect the tents on the school grounds, he declared, "We'll put them up anyway."

"You are not putting those tents up here," insisted the city's police commissioner, B. A. Hammond.

"We're raising these tents," Carmichael replied.

Police officers, their billy clubs drawn, surrounded Carmichael.

Hammond instructed an officer, "Frank, if he puts a hand on that tent, arrest him." Hammond's officers, all of whom were white men, watched as Carmichael moved forward. A representative of CORE and another SNCC organizer advanced, too.

Then they touched the tent.

Policemen immediately snapped handcuffs on the three activists, charged them with trespassing, and hauled them off to jail. The jailed leaders knew others would bail them out soon enough, and they'd be back

in the fray before long. Carmichael, gathering his strength for the work ahead, calmed down and went to sleep.

Meanwhile, marchers kept up their steady pace toward Greenwood. But even after walking more than 15 miles, they found themselves 5 miles short of their destination. Everyone piled into trucks and other vehicles, bound for town; volunteers would have to return the next day to close the missing miles on foot. After reaching the segregated part of Greenwood, activists began to occupy a neighborhood park for use as a campsite. Black residents gathered in support of the plan even as local policemen surrounded the block-size park, billy clubs clasped at the ready. This force was joined by an emergency contingent of highway patrolmen who'd been dispatched by the governor in response to the mayor's repeated pleas for aid.

A jubilant senior citizen rose to add his voice to a rally during the March Against Fear. Undated photo.

"Are you with us?" Green asked the crowd.

People shouted in support. Under the glare of the officers and amid the encouragement of the crowd, volunteers erected the night's tents in record time.

To the surprise of the activists, law enforcement personnel kept their distance. Local officials had changed their minds yet again. Instead of trying to exclude the marchers, the town would adopt the accommodating tone of previous town leaders, after all. Soon the local police chief was offering to adjust the park's lights for added security and to keep local whites out of the area. Outrage over the earlier arrests, the triumph of securing a campsite, the success of reaching Greenwood—a center of white power in the heart of the Mississippi Delta—all these factors fed a charged attitude among participants.

Plus there was that phrase African-American residents had been hearing repeatedly. A phrase that SNCC worker Willie Ricks had been testing for days around the delta. A phrase that SNCC hoped would accelerate the pace and direction of change within the civil rights movement. A phrase that Ricks had urged Carmichael to introduce to the world.

That night.

In Greenwood.

A phrase with two words.

"Black power."

From the beginning of the revived march, leaders had built energy and unity among marchers by chanting the movement's signature question: *What do you want?* And, mile after mile, marchers had answered the call by shouting one word: *FREEDOM!* Their reply to the follow-up question, *When do you want it?*, was always: *NOW!* Call and response. Call and response. One voice answered by many.

What do you want?

FREEDOM!

When do you want it?

NOW!

What do you want?

FREEDOM!

When do you want it?

NOW!

But Willie Ricks, working on behalf of SNCC, had begun proposing a new answer to the old question, a two-word alternative to the long-standing query *What do you want?*

Ricks tested the phrase with black people who lived in poverty throughout the delta. He tried it out with local blacks who lived in fear. He suggested it to folks whose skin color led them to be treated as second-class citizens.

His message was clear: *You folks don't just need freedom. You need power. Power for folks with black skin.*

With encouragement from Ricks, people began to answer the traditional call, *What do you want?*, with an entirely new response.

Those two words.

BLACK POWER!

By 1966, people had been marching for freedom for more than a decade, and, although it was true that they had made notable gains, blacks still lived at the margins of power. African Americans might be able to sit on the same seats as whites, drink from the same water fountains, and even begin to be permitted to vote in the same elections, but they were not their own keepers. One factor, and one factor alone, fueled that discrimination: skin color. If skin color mattered that much, then it was time for people with black skin to claim their rightful share of the white power structure.

It was time for black power.

**"If you think he's wrong,
you can't say it because he thinks
he's always right . . .
The only difference since slavery
is we're not sold like cattle."**

African-American woman from Drew,
commenting to a British reporter during the March Against Fear

**"We will live here with you
in the future as we have in the past
or we will fertilize the soil
of our beloved Southland
with your remains."**

Greenwood segregationists, writing after
witnessing the March Against Fear

"Each time the people in those cities saw Martin Luther King get slapped, they became angry; when they saw four little black girls bombed to death, they were angrier; and when nothing happened, they were steaming."

Stokely Carmichael, writing shortly after the March Against Fear about the frustrations that helped fuel race riots in U.S. cities

A police officer charged toward Stokely Carmichael when he attempted to erect a tent on the grounds of the segregated all-black elementary school in Greenwood on June 16.

CHAPTER 6

EARTHQUAKE

OLICE OFFICERS ARRESTED Stokely Carmichael in Greenwood, Mississippi, on the afternoon of June 16. A few hours later, hundreds of local blacks joined the marchers camped in Broad Street Park for the evening's civil rights rally. Organizers hosted such events in county seats to build participation at voter registration drives. Everyone anticipated a program of inspiring speeches and song, and local folks especially looked forward to hearing again from their good friend Stokely Carmichael. At least they looked forward to hearing from him if he got out of jail in time. Would he make it?

He did.

The crowd roared when Carmichael stepped onto the truck bed that doubled at events as a speaker's platform. Martin Luther King, Jr., was not in town that night, a circumstance that played to Carmichael's advantage. King, as the acknowledged head of the civil rights movement, always spoke last at events, in the place of honor. But not that night. That night, Thursday, June 16, 1966, Carmichael had the last word.

In reply to the cheers, he raised one arm with a clenched fist, then lowered it and began to talk. Carmichael spoke without notes, using a distinctive rhythm and diction that reflected three key geographical influences on his life: Trinidad, where he'd been born and spent his early childhood; New

DATE WALKED: June 17 **MILES WALKED:** 15 **ROUTE:** North of Greenwood to west of Greenwood

York City, where he'd lived as a teen; and the Deep South, where he'd perfected his activism.

After some soft-spoken words of greeting, Carmichael upped his volume.

"This is the 27th time I have been arrested, and I ain't going to jail no more. I ain't going to jail no more. The only way we gonna stop them white men from whuppin' us is to take over. We been saying, 'Freedom Now' for six years and we ain't got nothin'. What we gonna start saying now is 'black power.'"

"Don't be ashamed," urged Carmichael, and he began leading the crowd in a chant: "We want black power! We want black power! We want black power! We want black power! We want black power! We want black power! We want black power!" Seven times they repeated the phrase.

"That's right. That's what we want," he said. "Black power. And we don't have to be ashamed of it. We have stayed here, and we've begged the president. We've begged the federal government. That's all we've been doing. Begging and begging. We've done nothing but beg. We've got to stop begging and take power."

The park reverberated with cheers and applause.

"Ain't nothin' wrong with anything all black, 'cause I'm all black and I'm all good," Carmichael proclaimed. "The white folks in the state of Mississippi ain't nothing but a bunch of racists. Everybody owns our neighborhood except us. We outnumber the whites in this county; we want black power. That's what we want—black power!"

People cheered again as he added, "It's time we stand up and take over. Every courthouse in Mississippi oughta be burned down tomorrow to get rid of the dirt and the mess."

He continued: "Now from now on when they ask you what you want, you know what to tell them."

Willie Ricks leaped to the platform beside Carmichael and asked the crowd, "What do you want?" They shouted in reply: "BLACK POWER." Over and over the call and response echoed through the evening air.

"What do you want?"

"BLACK POWER!"

Carmichael delivered his historic speech about black power in Greenwood on the night of June 16.

"What do you want?"

"BLACK POWER!"

"Everybody, what do you want?"

"BLACK POWER!"

The cries hung in the air. Then Carmichael offered his conclusion.

"That's what we're gonna get."

Carmichael's call for black power slammed the March Against Fear with an intensity that rivaled—or even eclipsed—the force of Aubrey Norvell's shotgun blasts 10 days earlier. If the shooting of James Meredith had sent a tremor through the civil rights community,

Carmichael's speech felt like an earthquake. Nothing would be the same again. "We're watching history," SCLC photographer Bob Fitch observed while documenting Carmichael's speech.

King had been at work in Chicago on June 16 when he'd heard about Carmichael's detention. The arrest hadn't particularly surprised him. Local police had been "too polite" during the march so far, he had told a movement ally in New York City. It "just didn't feel like Mississippi." Carmichael's arrest felt normal; getting thrown in jail went hand in hand with activism in that state. But the news about Carmichael's black power speech—that got King's attention. SCLC aides on the ground in Greenwood urged him to return immediately to help manage the fallout from the provocative speech. Carmichael's words could be interpreted as a repudiation of the movement's devotion to the power of nonviolence, its reliance on interracial collaboration, its determination to build a community of equals. King rushed back to Mississippi.

It was time for damage control.

By the afternoon of Friday, June 17, the day after Carmichael's speech, King was addressing a rally outside the Leflore County courthouse in Greenwood. Without ever using the phrase "black power," King sought to define it within the traditions of the nonviolent struggle for civil rights. "Power is the ability to make the power structure say yes even when it wants to say no. The way to do this is to be voters," he insisted. "When we get this power, we will try to achieve a society of brotherhood," he promised.

His vision of brotherhood matched that of James Lawson and of other long-standing leaders in the civil rights movement. They sought to create what they called the "beloved community," a way of life akin to the lofty objectives expressed in King's "I Have a Dream" speech three years earlier. A brotherhood in which character trumped skin color and justice prevailed. But the phrase "black power" seemed out of step with this goal of peaceful coexistence.

Debates about the expression's meaning became personal for the participants in the March Against Fear. Just what was black power? And what did it mean for each of them? Younger blacks embraced the phrase more rapidly than their elders. Members of SNCC and CORE adopted the term faster than those allied with King and the SCLC. "We do need black power," agreed an SCLC associate, "but we don't need black power to take over and do to the white folks like they done to us."

Marchers loyal to tradition continued to ask for "freedom now" even as others took up the new SNCC chants of "black power" and "whites must go." Such calls seemed to signal the need for blacks to take charge of their movement for their own empowerment, and they unsettled the racial harmony that had marked both the march through Mississippi and the civil rights movement overall.

"If you say a couple of radical words around Northern white liberals, they cut off the money they been sending to the movement," observed James Phipps, a black Mississippian. "But we ain't going to win our freedom from the Southern white man and then lose it again to the Northern white man."

"Suddenly the happy feeling of the march was threatened," observed David Dawley, a white student from the University of Michigan. "Suddenly I felt threatened." The young man added: "It seemed like a hit on well-intentioned northern whites like me, that the message from Willie Ricks was, 'Go home, white boy, we don't need you.'" Relinquishing responsibility for black empowerment to the blacks themselves "seemed like the logical conclusion to what the movement had been about," decided Dick Reavis, a white organizer for the SCLC.

The roots of the idea of black power had been set long before the walk to Jackson. Such luminaries as W. E. B. DuBois, Richard Wright, and Malcolm X had championed the need for black empowerment for years. In 1964, Malcolm X began delivering a speech he called "The Ballot or the Bullet," urging whites to share voting rights with blacks before frustrations over black oppression led to violence. "Give it to us now," he advised. "Don't wait for next year. Give it to us yesterday, and that's not fast enough." A year later, Malcolm X's voice was silenced in a bloody assassination. Frustration over his death and his unfulfilled demands had contributed to a growing hunger among SNCC activists for measurable social change. Desires for launching a SNCC movement for black power had been brewing ever since.

When Carmichael unveiled his organization's call for black power during his speech in Greenwood, even his use of the word "black" created controversy. Slaves and their descendants had been criticized by whites for having dark skin all their lives, been mistreated because of their skin color, been insulted with phrases that linked their skin color with racial slurs, such as "black bastard," until the word itself felt tainted. Racist whites had made being black seem bad. A negative. Something one lived with more than celebrated. Members of the African-American community had spent generations fighting to be called "Negroes" or other terms of respect, and "black" was not one of them. Yet here was Carmichael using the word with pride, infusing it with possibilities, suggesting that being black was a good thing, not something to be constrained by or ashamed of.

Among young people, especially, it became cutting edge to call oneself black. The term "Negro," which

Journalists pooled their funds and rented a truck that proceeded slowly ahead of the marchers to make it easier to film and photograph the walk. They hiked alongside the marchers, too, and even flew overhead, capturing aerial views of the procession. Undated photo.

had stood for decades as the preferred racial descriptor, suddenly seemed dated, old-fashioned. Terminology that had evolved from "colored people" to "Negro" began shifting once again as individuals began self-identifying as black, and the word "Negro" faded quickly from use. Before long, the term "African American" joined "black" as the racial identifiers of preference. Decades later, "people of color" would join the lexicon as a way to refer to individuals from a variety of ethnic and racial backgrounds.

If the use of the word "black" created challenges, pairing it with the politically charged word "power" further intensified its shock value. The phrase was just edgy enough to engage a younger generation growing weary of the slow pace of change: *Could black power take the fight to the next level and bring about a social revolution?* It was just vague enough to alarm some whites: *Wouldn't more power for blacks mean less power for whites?* It was just militant enough to sound like a repudiation of the power of nonviolence: *Was Carmichael issuing a call to arms? Just what was "black power," anyway?*

During the previous five years, the news media had been an essential advocate for the civil rights movement, ready to risk life and limb in order to cover breaking news of white-on-black violence during courageous nonviolent protests. "If it hadn't been for the media—the print media and television—the civil rights movement would have been like a bird without wings, a choir without a song," as John Lewis, a civil rights pioneer and Carmichael's predecessor as SNCC chair, would later say.

Just the previous year, the news media had documented the violent attack by state troopers on Lewis and others on the Edmund Pettus Bridge in their first attempt to march from Selma to Montgomery. The reports offered undeniable proof of regional oppression, and they had helped galvanize support for civil rights. But the idea of black power undermined the long-standing alliance between the movement and the media. The term confused and unsettled many of the on-site white reporters. Journalists scrambled to define the term even before Carmichael and other movement leaders could do so. And their accounts, instead of helping the civil rights movement, began to hurt it.

"Perhaps the reason for the disproportionate emphasis on divisive issues during the march was that civil-rights news—like news of any unified, protracted struggle against injustice—becomes boring," speculated Renata Adler in the *New Yorker* after covering the March Against Fear. "One march, except to marchers, is very like another. Tents, hot days, worried nights, songs, rallies, heroes, villains, even tear gas and clubbing—the props are becoming stereotyped."

Carmichael's speech gave reporters an opening to write about something new, and they pounced on his demand for black power. Journalists portrayed the phrase as a bit dangerous, a bit scary, a bit rebellious. "Black power" was "a racist philosophy," charged *Time* magazine. It was a "battle cry of racial alienation," *Newsweek* magazine suggested. As civil rights historian Taylor Branch notes in the American Experience documentary *Citizen King*, white news reporters "seized on" the phrase. To them "it essentially says, 'There is a war coming.' Black people are about to make war." As a result, the concept of black power took on an outsize meaning. Some reporters began referring to its supporters as militants, a term that reinforced the idea that "black power" was somehow a cry for a violent uprising.

And, really, hadn't such violence already begun?

In the years leading up to the March Against Fear, journalists had reported the waves of race riots that were breaking out around the country. Even as King and others continued to champion the power of nonviolence, cities began to erupt with violence. In Harlem and other neighborhoods in New York City during 1964, triggered by the fatal shooting of a black youth by an off-duty white policeman. In the Watts area of Los Angeles in 1965, where abusive police behavior during a routine traffic stop escalated into a six-day riot that killed 34, injured more than 1,000, and left much of the neighborhood in flames. There had been unrest in other cities since 1964, too, and race riots had already begun again in 1966.

Blacks trapped in urban ghettos of concentrated poverty were turning to violence. Blacks harassed by white police officers and white merchants were turning to violence. Reporters wondered, could activists in the civil rights movement turn violent next? Such coverage made their readers consider the same possibility. Two years after the march, SNCC veteran and future children's author Julius Lester summed up the nation's reaction to black power with a provocatively titled book, *Look Out, Whitey! Black*

As marchers hiked beyond Greenwood on June 17, they passed a truck parked beside the road that was heavily laden with cotton—a substance intimately entwined with the lives of generations of southern blacks.

Power's Gon' Get Your Mama! Recalling the phrase's debut, Lester wrote, "All the whites wanted to know was if Black Power was antiwhite and if it meant killing white folks. The nation was hysterical."

If reporters had dug a little deeper, they would have recognized why the new expression caught fire. "Of course they chanted for black power," explains Aram Goudsouzian, historian and author of the definitive account of the March Against Fear. The expression fit their situation perfectly because, as he writes in *Down to the Crossroads,* "they were poor, they were black, and they had no power."

But what was supposed to be a march against fear was starting to stir up more anxieties than ever, and the news media played an essential role in that. After the press's initial reaction to Carmichael's speech in Greenwood and to the "black power" phrase, activists already wary around reporters became even more so. "Nobody in camp trusted them," observed one participant. "They never really told the outside world what the whole thing was all about." Carmichael became prickly with the news media, perhaps resentful that a movement for black rights depended on a press pool that was overwhelmingly white. "I don't think the newsmen can interpret me," he had said after his speech in Greenwood on June 16. "They aren't black."

A distance settled between Carmichael and the reporters he'd once worked with easily. Carmichael said provocative things, but was cagey about their meanings. Did he really think that the courthouses of Mississippi should be burned to the ground? Sometimes he assured reporters that his language had been a metaphor, other times, he seemed to have really meant it. Such interactions with the media just fed the beast, and the subsequent reporting reflected—and further fueled—his angry tone.

"The Student Nonviolent Coordinating Committee is speaking about the right of black people to have power in the counties where they outnumber whites who are racist, that they control those governments," Carmichael explained to one television reporter. "That's what every other ethnic group in this country has done, and the people who oppose that are anti-black."

Although a radical concept given how disenfranchised blacks were, his logic was hard to dispute. Yet, when the reporter asked where Carmichael stood on the subject of violence, he replied: "I stand mute." In other words, Carmichael wouldn't say one way or the other if his organization—which, after all, had the very word nonviolent in its name—approved the idea of using violent means to achieve black power. When Carmichael complained to a SNCC staffer in New York about the press's depiction of black power being a call for violence, she urged him to stop giving such "juicy quotes. Be a little more boring." But Carmichael had no interest in being boring. He had other priorities.

He wanted black power.

The phrase echoed along the highway on Friday, June 17, the day after his speech, as Carmichael and others led about 100 marchers back into Greenwood, completing the five-mile stretch of highway that they'd covered the previous day in vehicles. And it rang out again after dinner when some 150 people hiked the first 10 miles of the highway that led toward the delta town of Itta Bena.

Or, actually, two phrases competed for top billing during those marches and at other events throughout the day: one long-standing and one brand-new.

Racial tensions in Mississippi during June 1966 remained on a hair trigger that could ignite into violence with little or no provocation.

What do you want?
FREEDOM!
When do you want it?
NOW!
What do you want?
FREEDOM!
When do you want it?
NOW!
Call and response. Call and response.
What do you want?
BLACK POWER!
What do you want?
BLACK POWER!
What do you want?
BLACK POWER!

In the days that followed Carmichael's speech in Greenwood, King continued to make his case for achieving racial harmony through the power of nonviolence. "I don't care if every Negro in the United States comes down and urges using violence," he told supporters in Detroit on Saturday, June 18. "I will still be the last one to cry against it." King avoided even saying the phrase, and the continued competition between the calls for *freedom now* and *black power* distressed him.

Carmichael sought to define the quest for black power in constructive terms. Black votes created black power, he said. Black power created a sense of self-worth. "That doesn't mean we're anti-white," he explained the day after his Greenwood speech. "We are just developing pride." But Carmichael continued to express his anger and frustration in provocative ways that competed with his message. "The only way that black people in Mississippi will create an attitude where they will not be shot down like pigs, where they will not be shot down like dogs, is when they get the power where they constitute a majority in counties to institute justice," he told a reporter two days after the speech.

"I think it scared people because they did not understand [it]," Floyd McKissick said of the phrase "black power" years later. "They could not subtract violence from power. They could only see power as having a violent instrument accompanying it."

Black power scared white people, and black folks tended to suffer when white folks felt afraid.

"It is time to stop being ashamed of being black. It is time to stop trying to be white. When you see your daughter playing in the fields, with her nappy hair, and her wide nose, and her thick lips, tell her she is beautiful. *Tell your daughter she is beautiful."*

Stokely Carmichael, speaking to locals during the March Against Fear

"They can pass all the laws they want, but niggers'll still have black faces. Where's this gonna end? I'll tell you. It's gonna end when we mow 'em down, mow 'em down."

White customer in a Grenada barbershop, commenting on the March Against Fear

"Ain't gonna let nobody turn me 'round,
Turn me 'round, turn me 'round,
Ain't gonna let nobody turn me 'round.
I'm gonna keep on a-walkin', keep on a-talkin',
Marching up to freedom land."

A traditional spiritual turned protest song

A deputy sheriff shoved the SCLC's Hosea Williams (wearing plaid shirt) off the lawn of the county courthouse in Greenwood on June 17 when organizers tried to hold a voter registration rally on the grass. Eventually officers permitted participants to congregate on the building's steps and sidewalk.

CHAPTER 7

WHITE RAGE

N UNEASY TENSION PERSISTED as marchers struck their campsite and left Greenwood on Saturday, June 18. Although their stay in the county seat had prompted local blacks to register, not enough had done so to secure an African-American voting majority. Still, it was a start. "The people are moving with us now," observed Mississippi activist Fannie Lou Hamer. "And even those who don't register this week are at least beginning to think about it for the first time."

A string of long, hot marches lay ahead for participants, hikes through tiny towns that survived on cotton. Itta Bena. Quito. Morgan City. Pugh City. Belzoni. Silver City. Midnight. Louise. Campsites were hard to come by in the sparsely populated region, so the group spent two nights on the grounds of Green Grove Baptist Church in Belzoni, the next county seat on their path, and relied on vehicles to transport them to and from their route. Next they camped near Louise on the farm of Hura Montgomery, an African American whose ancestors had been able to acquire land following the Civil War.

Wherever they slept, marchers gathered together for rallies at night and urged locals to register by day. People came and went, including an interracial group from Chicago that traveled overnight by bus to contribute several days of legwork to the effort. Rival chants

DATES WALKED: June 18–20 **MILES WALKED:** 46 **ROUTE:** West of Greenwood to Louise

continued to fill the air. "The conflict quite obviously wasn't going to be solved yet," observed one of the Chicagoans, Stanley Plona, a veteran of previous civil rights protests.

Progress for the daily effort was measured in numbers—how many miles walked, how many voters registered, how many days to go—but there were personal yardsticks, too. How many days since the last shower? How many days since the last shave? Would it be even hotter tomorrow? Would there be any shade along the route? Was it going to rain? Who had fallen in love? Who had broken up? Did everyone else's feet hurt, too? Would their shoes outlast the walk? How much worse could the body odor get?

Ever changing combinations of civil rights leaders walked together during the March Against Fear (in this case, from left, Bernard Lee and Martin Luther King, Jr., from the SCLC, and Stokely Carmichael and Willie Ricks of SNCC). Undated photo.

And still they had to answer that persistent question: What do you want? Occasionally new variations appeared in their answers. Tommy Johnson, a three-year-old Canadian marching with his parents, refused to choose between freedom and black power. He knew exactly what he wanted: "A kitty cat!" After hiking 17.5 miles to reach the Montgomery farm, marchers had a new request, too: "A little rest!"

Bits of outside news punctuated the daily marching routine. On June 17, Aubrey Norvell, the gunman who'd shot James Meredith, was released on bail. Norvell's lawyers had secured the $25,000 required for him to leave jail, pending trial in November. Questions of motive and logic remained a mystery; Norvell and his wife went into seclusion without comment.

Two days later, on Sunday, June 19, Meredith was back in the media spotlight, as was Stokely Carmichael. The men appeared on separate news shows, where panels of journalists peppered them with questions during live interviews on national TV—Carmichael on CBS's *Face the Nation* and Meredith on NBC's *Meet the Press*. On each program, the reporters seemed determined to cast their guests as militant counterforces to the King-led movement of nonviolent protest. Meredith suggested that the phrase "black power" seemed no different in purpose to him than other movement chants or the singing of the protest anthem "We Shall Overcome." Both men spoke supportively of nonviolence, but both refused to condemn violence categorically. "I think that the non-violence is fine, but I don't think it can ever go far enough," said Meredith, observing that violence seemed to be an integral part of the national character and its history.

Carmichael's invitation to appear on *Face the Nation* demonstrated how his black power speech had elevated him to the national stage. His stature already had increased the month before when he'd taken over the chairmanship of SNCC by unseating John Lewis, a revered proponent of nonviolent protest, in a controversial vote. Since then, Carmichael had encouraged the group's more radical shift toward black power. Now he became, to the news media, the counterweight to Martin Luther King, Jr. He was a younger, more aggressive champion for change, a successor to the recently slain Malcolm X. King seemed to convey the voice of tradition, Carmichael the call of the radical.

Reporters focused on the idea that there was a war brewing between the leaders of the civil rights movement. Black power was splintering the movement into rival camps, they suggested. Carmichael versus King. Revolution versus tradition. *Black power* versus *freedom now*. They portrayed the two men as a study in contrasts, a source for conflict. Conflict was good, when it came to reporting. Conflict sold papers. Conflict boosted ratings.

News reporters minimized the factors the men shared in common—from their commitment to fight for racial equality to their determination to reach Jackson—and emphasized their differences instead. The tensions conveyed by the media helped to foster actual tensions within the march, which thus reinforced continued reporting on tension in a repetitive loop. But Carmichael and King didn't see conflict or tension as the focus of their relationship. They'd worked as allies in the movement for years, and each man admired and drew inspiration from the other.

King, at 37, enjoyed Carmichael's youthful energy and tenacity. Carmichael, at 24, was just slightly younger than King had been when he had gained national prominence through his leadership during the Montgomery bus boycott. Like King, Carmichael had a sharp mind. He'd majored in philosophy in college. He was a fierce debater. The two men enjoyed the challenge of matching their intellects. Carmichael looked up to King even if, at times, they locked horns over particulars. King was fearless. A brilliant strategist. A mentor. A few days after making his black power speech in Greenwood, Carmichael admitted to King that he had used his friend, had "deliberately decided to raise this issue on the march in order to give it a national forum, and to force you to take a stand on black power." King laughed. "I have been used before," he said. "One more time won't hurt."

But King realized that by introducing black power during the March Against Fear, Carmichael had changed the tone of the discourse. About the protest. About the goal of coexisting harmoniously as equals regardless of race. About the way forward. Carmichael had disrupted the camaraderie of their protest and changed its focus. "Because Stokely Carmichael chose the march as an arena for a debate over black power," King observed to a reporter, "we didn't get to emphasize the evils of Mississippi and the need for the 1966 Civil Rights Act. Internal dissension along the march helped Mississippi get off the hook somewhat."

King began to question the merits of the march. Maybe they shouldn't have even undertaken it. Before long he would suggest privately that it had been a mistake. The walk was becoming endless. And sprawling. And expensive. Would they ever be able to raise enough money to pay for it all? Media coverage of the effort created more controversy than support. The movement seemed to be fracturing right before their eyes.

And every day brought new disasters.

The next morning, on Tuesday, June 21, 1966, members of the March Against Fear made another diversion from the main route. This time recent events, not voter registration, motivated their trip. Exactly two years earlier on June 21, 1964, near Philadelphia, Mississippi, local police had arrested three young civil rights workers for an alleged traffic violation and locked them in jail. Then they disappeared. The police said they'd freed the men that night. If true, the trio had returned to the road at a time when white supremacists often committed acts of terrorism and violence. Missing were a 21-year-old black Mississippian named James Chaney and two whites from New York, Andrew Goodman, age 20, and Michael Schwerner, 24. They had been helping CORE with its 1964 Freedom Summer project.

Friends, family, and coworkers feared the worst. Carmichael, based in Greenwood that summer, was among those involved in early searches for the missing men. Forty-four days would elapse before FBI agents located their bodies buried within the walls of a new earthen dam a few miles outside of Philadelphia. All suspicions pointed to the region's Ku Klux Klan, whose members included local police officers. Among the prime suspects were Cecil Price, the deputy sheriff who had arrested the activists, and his boss, Sheriff Lawrence Rainey. But the wheels of justice turned slowly for such cases during that era in the South, and neither they nor anyone else had yet been held accountable for the murders in the past two years.

With the March Against Fear taking place in the same state during the second anniversary of the activists' disappearance, civil rights leaders agreed that, in memory of the fallen and in a show of solidarity, King and a delegation of other marchers would travel to Philadelphia, which was east of Highway 51, for a commemorative gathering. On Tuesday morning this group of some 20 people joined more than 200 local blacks for a prearranged march from Mt. Nebo Baptist Church, in the segregated section of the community, to the Neshoba County courthouse, about a mile away in downtown Philadelphia. When the group set out, they shouted civil rights slogans to reinforce strength and unity, and they sang a traditional spiritual that had become a protest song of the movement, "Ain't Gonna Let Nobody Turn Me 'Round."

After marchers left the relative safety of the black neighborhood, vehicles filled with angry whites began to buzz past them and swerve toward them before stopping suddenly. One passenger swung a wooden club in their direction from a speeding vehicle. Others shouted race-based insults during an era when such hateful expressions found their way routinely into public speech. "I wouldn't dirty my Goddamned car with you black bastards!" screamed a young woman, using one of the period's offensive racial

When a car charged a group of marchers, they scattered in self-defense. Undated photo.

slurs, one that had helped to connect the very word "black" to feelings of shame and disgrace.

Fewer than a dozen local policemen were on the scene, and they showed little interest in intervening. The law enforcement officers in Philadelphia hadn't sought backup help from state troopers, and only one state patrol squad was at hand. Even the county sheriff was absent, so Deputy Cecil Price assumed charge, alongside the city's police chief. But plenty of local whites were on alert—several hundred of them, in fact. Lining the street as marchers approached. Hanging out of second story windows. Perching in trees and on rooftops. Watching to see what happened next.

Not for the first or last time would King and other leaders walk with their followers into the face of death.

First they stopped outside the county jail where Chaney, Goodman, and Schwerner had been detained. A cluster of local police officers stood by as dozens of white men temporarily trapped King's group by congregating at each end of the city block where the jailhouse stood. The marchers knelt to pray. It was a symbolic act, and also a fortifying one, but whites drowned out the prayers and speeches with sounds of their own. Car horns and revving engines. Insults, curses, and threats.

Threats screamed in rage.

Threats screamed in hatred.

And, on some level, threats screamed in fear.

For many southern whites, seeing such acts of black bravery defied the natural order of their world. Blacks were supposed to be afraid of whites, subservient to whites, inferior to whites. Evidence to the contrary frightened whites, and it fueled a rage that reflected patterns of violent oppression laid down over centuries. The whips of slavery's overseers might have faded into history, but a determination to remain superior using force and terror had lived on through the generations. Ropes became nooses, crosses burned menacingly, and guns proved deadly. Lynchings and shootings. White hoods and indiscriminate arrest. Such acts were supposed to keep blacks in their place.

And now they were not.

On that day in Philadelphia, anticipating the protesters' show of defiant, peaceful solidarity, many whites resorted to arms once again in a desperate attempt to restore their place of racial supremacy. They carried clubs. They brought switchblades. They grabbed ordinary household items that could double as menacing weapons. A garden hoe, chains, wrenches. Ax handles, pliers, knives.

King and the others pressed past the white assembly and proceeded toward the courthouse. Deputy Price refused to let them enter the courthouse grounds, so they gathered for their memorial service on the street before it. Local whites, who slightly outnumbered the protesters, encircled King and the others, unrestrained by law enforcement officers.

"This is the day he will die," thought Roy Reed, who was covering the event for the *New York Times*. King's national stature made him target number one for violence. Indeed, his presence upped the stakes for everyone taking part in the event, including the visiting news reporters whom segregationists resented for their ability to turn local events into national news.

Speakers competed to make themselves heard above the crush of crowd noise. King raised his voice to recall the slain civil rights workers: "I believe in my heart that the murderers are somewhere around me at this moment."

A white boy in the crowd shouted: "They're right behind you!" a claim that brought chuckles and hoots from the bystanders.

King challenged the whites by saying, "We are not afraid. If they kill three of us, they will have to kill all of us."

He continued speaking, despite the noise of the crowd. Firecrackers exploded nearby, and yet he persevered. Nonviolence in the face of violence. Dignity over anarchy. Justice over injustice. Love in answer to hate.

"The Lord is my shepherd; I shall not want," he prayed, reciting verses from Psalm 23 that had routed terror from the hearts of nonviolent protesters many times before. The psalm proclaimed: "Yea, though I walk through the valley of the shadow of death, I will fear no evil: for thou art with me."

Then the marchers walked back.

Back through the gauntlet of screaming whites. Back along the dusty road that led to the black side of town. Back past whites who hurled stones at the marchers, hurled soft drink bottles at them, hurled eggs at them. Back toward the sanctuary of their church as whites attacked newsmen, wrenched bulky television equipment off their shoulders, wrestled two white journalists to the ground. Back through the valley of death even as the discipline of nonviolence frayed, and blacks began to return punches, and a brawl started to gain momentum. Only then did the police step in, separate the fighters, and ratchet back the tension just enough for the procession to complete its journey.

King's brave facade gave way as the threat receded. He had been afraid back at the courthouse, more afraid, he would later admit, than at any earlier time in the movement. "This is a terrible town, the worst I've seen," he told reporters. "There is a complete reign of terror here." Within hours of the experience, he and others concluded there was only one reasonable way to respond to their treatment, one way to counter the hate speech, one way to protest the violent and menacing crowd. There was only one possible way to demonstrate that the power of nonviolence, the power of love, was greater than hate, greater than fear.

They'd have to go back and do it again.

"I am not afraid of any man,
whether he is in Mississippi or Michigan,
whether he is in Birmingham or Boston.
I am not afraid of any man."

Martin Luther King, Jr., speaking in
Philadelphia, Mississippi, on June 21, 1966

"Hey, Luther!
Thought you wasn't scared of anybody.
Come up here alone and prove it."

Heckler addressing Martin Luther King, Jr., during his speech
in Philadelphia, Mississippi, June 21, 1966

"They don't call it* white *power. They just call it* power. *I'm committed to non-violence, but I say what we need is to get us some* black *power."

Floyd McKissick of CORE, following the confrontation with state troopers in Canton, Mississippi

A fog of tear gas enveloped a ball field in Canton on June 23, as state troopers attacked marchers trying to camp there.

CHAPTER 8

SUPREMACY

VEN AS ORGANIZERS made plans to return to Philadelphia later in the week, they had to keep moving toward Jackson. An already complicated and unwieldy operation just kept growing more and more complex. On the morning of Tuesday, June 21, the core of marchers had continued walking through the delta while Martin Luther King, Jr., and associates made their initial trip to Philadelphia. They'd hiked 18.5 miles and reached another county seat by day's end, Yazoo City. Once again they received a grudging welcome.

Town leaders and members of the local White Citizens' Council had decided to follow the same just-put-up-with-it-and-they'll-leave-soon strategy of earlier county seats, and, as a result, they had agreed to allow the marchers to camp in a public park. The facility's whites-only swimming pool held no water, probably in order to prevent its integration. But the park did have showers, a welcomed reward for marchers after multiple days of sweaty hiking.

Yazoo City marked a turning point, literally, for the march through Mississippi. Hikers had passed the westernmost point on their delta diversion and were, at last, heading east. Canton—and the return to Highway 51—lay just two days and 35 miles away. Three days after Canton, they'd reach Jackson.

They were entering the homestretch.

DATES WALKED: June 21–23 **MILES WALKED:** 53 **ROUTE:** Louise to Canton

That evening, hundreds of local blacks gathered, as they had done at stops all along the route, to hear speeches by King and others. But rallies that had built unity early in the march were becoming public debates about the nature of the civil rights movement. The right to self-defense versus a steadfast commitment to nonviolence. A shifting focus on black power versus continued emphasis on seeking brotherhood between races. That night, as the final speaker, King found himself challenged once again with tying up the tangled threads of various speeches into some statement of solidarity.

It had been a long day for the movement leader. A long, tough day. The trip to Philadelphia might have seemed like enough work already, but King had traveled from there to a distant voter registration rally in Indianola, the judicial seat for Sunflower County. Then he had rushed to catch up with the main march in Yazoo City. Even so, King still found the reserves to deliver a triumphant defense that evening of the power of nonviolence.

"Somebody said tonight that we are in a majority," King reminded the crowd. "Don't fool yourself. We are not in a majority in a single state in the United States." He continued: "We are ten percent of the population of this nation, and it would be foolish for me to stand up and tell you we are going to get freedom by ourselves."

He built an argument for the power of nonviolence, step by step. "The weakness of violence from our side," he said, is that violence "can always be halted by superior force. But," said King, "we have another method, and I've seen it, and they can't stop it."

King reminded listeners of past triumphs from the nonviolent movement. Then he went on. "I'm disturbed about a strange theory that is circulating, saying to me that I ought to imitate the worst in the white man and the worst in our presence. Who has a history of killing and lynching people and throwing them in rivers? It is our oppressors. And now people are telling me to stoop down to that level. Oh, no."

A voice from the crowd echoed his call—"Oh, no!"—and applause rippled through the gathering.

"That I will not do." King declared. "That is the reason I'm not gonna allow anybody to pull me so low as to use the very methods that perpetuated evil throughout our civilization." King listed all the ways power had worked to human disadvantage: "I am sick and tired of power. I'm tired of the war in Vietnam. I'm tired of war and conflict in the world. I'm tired of shooting. I'm tired of hate. I'm tired of selfishness. I'm tired of evil. I'm not going to use violence no matter who says it." The crowd cheered enthusiastically.

He'd pulled them back from the brink.

But King had reached his limit. He called a meeting of march leaders for the next day. It was time to unify their message. The group debated for five hours on Wednesday without breaking the deadlock. Stokely Carmichael and Floyd McKissick continued to support the use of the phrase "black power" during the march; King did not. Finally he asked those gathered if they would at least stop leading competing chants. They agreed. It was a subtle change, but it helped.

On the afternoon of Wednesday, June 22, more than 100 local blacks registered at the Yazoo County courthouse. Then the hikers resumed their eastward march, covering 13 miles of roadway to reach the hamlet of Benton, the last stop on their delta detour. The next day, 50 of the hardiest marchers completed a hot and stormy 20-plus-mile trek to Canton. During the final miles on Thursday, their shoes touched the pavement of Highway 51 for the first time in eight days. Marchers began singing as they entered the Madison County seat, and a crowd of about 1,500 local blacks greeted them at the courthouse and gathered for speeches.

Meanwhile, all day a controversy had been building in Canton over a routine question: Where would the marchers sleep? Organizers wanted to use public land—demonstrating their rights to equal access of tax-supported spaces—but the leaders of Canton refused. The public parks in the community had been closed for some time in order to prevent locals from integrating them, and they weren't about to reopen them for activists. With marchers en route to Canton, volunteers tried to occupy the grounds of all-black McNeal Elementary School, but local officials shooed them away even though a highway patrol commander had initially endorsed the idea. When a fresh contingent of volunteers began setting up their canvas tents at the same spot, Canton police officers arrested them.

To the leaders of the march, the situation in Canton seemed to mirror the one they had faced in Greenwood. They had pushed back and prevailed there. Why not do so again? They felt they were acting within their rights to use public property and that local officials were discriminating against them by refusing to accommodate their requests. So they persevered once more.

"They said we couldn't pitch our tents on *our* black school," an outraged Carmichael told the crowd that welcomed marchers at the county courthouse. "Well, we're going to do it *now*!" He helped lead the crowd through the segregated streets of Canton toward the neighborhood elementary school. Hundreds of local blacks swelled the ranks until as many as 3,500 people occupied the school's ball field. The sun had already set for the day, so volunteers worked by flashlight to begin erecting the tents.

Unbeknownst to organizers, city officials remained determined to reject the movement's argument for equal access to public spaces, and they had requested state troopers to help impose their decision. The governor agreed to support the city's position and urged a forceful response. A convoy of state patrol cars reached the school grounds while activists were setting up their tents. Seventy-five officers spilled out of the vehicles, heavily armed and wearing protective helmets, but they did not immediately intervene. Some locals, sensing trouble, began melting into the shadows and disappeared. Still, more than 2,000 people remained on the field, and the tent raising continued.

"You will not be allowed to erect that tent on this lot," interrupted the city attorney, who had reached the scene. "If you continue doing so you will be placed under arrest."

Civil rights leaders had heard similar warnings countless times before. They'd faced arrest and been jailed repeatedly during nonviolent protests, and they would go to jail, again, if they had to, to advocate for their right to use public property. The troopers seemed prepared to eject them forcibly from the school grounds, though, so first-time protesters from Canton needed quick coaching on how to protect themselves with the principles of nonviolence. "When we say lock arms, lock arms," McKissick instructed the crowd, having climbed atop a truck to gain their attention. "When we say sit down, sit down."

"I want to get this over because this is important," added King, who had joined McKissick on top of the truck's cab. King tried to instill the crowd with courage: "We're gonna stick together. If necessary, we are willing to fill up all of the jails in the state of Mississippi. And I don't believe they have enough jails to hold all of us people if they start arresting us!"

Carmichael, standing with King and McKissick, led chants of, "We're gonna pitch the tents! We're gonna pitch the tents! We're gonna pitch the tents!" Others shouted: "Freedom! Freedom!"

"Take out your handkerchiefs," urged McKissick, who could see that the officers were armed with tear gas. During an era when folks still carried handkerchiefs in their pockets, such a request was easy to follow. "Put them over your face," McKissick instructed.

Two minutes after the warning to cease the tent raising, troopers began firing gas canisters at the assembly. Some canisters carried conventional tear gas; others carried a toxic mix of irritating substances that made a person's skin feel as if it were on fire. People began to scream and cry. Shouts of "No, no!" mingled with the calls of "Freedom!" and "We're gonna pitch the tents!"

"Nobody leave," shouted King. "Nobody fight back. We're going to stand our ground," and he began singing "We Shall Overcome" as chaos enveloped the scene.

People couldn't see because it was dark. People couldn't see because of the clouds of gas spreading across the field. People couldn't see because the tear gas triggered intense watering of the eyes. The gases produced a toxic smell and made it hard to breathe. People's skin began to burn from the chemical agents in the gas. "My whole body felt blistered," one participant later recalled. "My scalp felt like every hair was being pulled out one by one, and my lungs as though I was inhaling molten steel."

Law enforcement officers typically use tear gas to disperse a crowd, launching canisters in a pattern that herds people out of an area. But not that night. That night the state troopers drenched the entire field with chemicals. They weren't trying to disperse people, it became clear; they were trying to hurt them. For weeks now, cadres of white highway patrolmen had been accompanying these marchers as they'd walked through Mississippi, listening in as they shared a message that must have become increasingly offensive to many of the men during a time and place where law officers sympathized frequently with the Ku Klux Klan. That anger may have simmered, building mile by mile, speech by speech, chant by chant. That night it reached its boiling point. Here was their chance to assert supremacy.

Troopers wearing protective gas masks advanced on the crowd and fired canisters toward people who were fleeing. They fired canisters toward people trapped against a school building wall. They aimed them at organizers shouting directions from their perch on the camp truck. Carmichael and McKissick were both hit. They fired canisters under the flaps of a recently erected tent, then pulled out its supportive stakes, trapping the people who'd sought shelter there in a canvas chamber of poisonous air.

Not satisfied, troopers began physically attacking individuals who remained on the field. The victims included several dozen of the most steadfast protesters, veterans of the movement who had dropped to the ground when the teargassing began, knowing this zone would be relatively free of the rising vapors. They were prepared to protest in place and face arrest. But arrests didn't come. A reporter at the scene observed, "At one point, an eerie silence enveloped the field, punctuated only by what sounded like men kicking footballs; it was the hollow clunk of cops kicking and clubbing fallen marchers." The attacks were indiscriminate. Women. Young people. Older people. A clergyman. Whites. Blacks. A one-legged marcher named Jim Leatherer. A youth who was vomiting from the effects of the gas. Screams and moans mixed with the THUD, THUD, THUD of guns striking against human beings.

Tear gas swirled inside a tent where marchers had sought shelter. "It was like a scene of hell," observed one of the journalists who witnessed the attack in Canton on June 23.

Then officers roughly dragged the people from the field.

They arrested no one.

Within half an hour, the attack was over; troopers had cleared the school grounds. Highway patrolmen confiscated the camp tents and drove away, leaving behind the wounded and a community of people teetering between rage and horror. Between agony and sorrow. Between violence and nonviolence.

City officials defended their call for reinforcements. To them, it had been essential to suppress an act of racial defiance. "Suppose they got away with this," the county attorney said of the camping effort. "They would want to take City Hall next." Mississippi's governor minimized the severity of the attack and called the use of tear gas "the humane thing to do."

Carmichael, who had lost more than one friend to white-on-black

State troopers "were not arresting, they were punishing," observed one of the journalists in Canton on June 23.

violence during his time in the movement, had become frantic during the confrontation, afraid that someone might die that night. "Don't make your stand here," he had begun to sob. "I just can't stand to see any more people shot." The situation stirred the peaceable McKissick to verbal fury. "I'm tired of having to *negotiate* for our Constitutional *rights,*" he declared.

When reporters asked King if the Canton attack had shaken his faith in nonviolence, he replied, "Oh, not at all." He countered: "How could we be violent in the midst of a police force like that?" But King knew such attacks made it harder to argue against the most aggressive dimensions of black power. "The government has got to give me some victories if I'm going to keep people nonviolent."

Organizers struggled to pull order out of the night's wreckage. Local blacks who lived near the school helped victims rinse their eyes and skin with garden hoses. At least one local woman had received such a toxic dousing of gas that layers of skin had peeled off her face. A dozen or more protesters had been overcome by gas fumes and passed out, including the three-year-old boy from Canada, Tommy Johnson. All of them recovered. Two local churches, one Methodist and one Catholic, opened their doors to the scattered marchers, feeding them and offering them places to sleep. Nuns helped tend to the injured, for even members of the medical crew

Makeshift medical care followed the ferocious attack in Canton, including checking pulses and treating eyes for exposure to tear gas.

traveling with the march had been hurt during the attack.

Traumatized participants regrouped in a church sanctuary to hear rallying speeches and to sing songs. Leaders announced plans to protest the attack with the power of nonviolence. Their first act would be a march through the streets of Canton just before midnight, singing protest songs of solidarity. Five hundred people braved the darkness in a protest march through the town and returned to the church without incident. Movement leaders also suggested that residents boycott white-owned businesses in Canton and stay home from work for a day, a not insignificant punishment for local whites who depended on blacks for childcare, as maids, as handymen, and more. And they planned to try again to camp on the schoolhouse grounds the next evening.

Still, it had been a tough day during a tough week. Cursed and threatened in Philadelphia on Tuesday. Gassed and beaten in Canton on Thursday. True, they expected to be in Jackson by Sunday, but that was three days away. What else could go wrong? Could things get any worse? It certainly seemed possible.

Tomorrow they'd be marching again in Philadelphia.

As the leaders prepared to defend the power of nonviolence by returning to Philadelphia, they did so with a noticeable lack of federal interest.

In earlier years, national officials had expressed outrage over violent racial attacks and had condemned the oppressive use of force by state and local law officers. They had intervened with political pressure, federal personnel, and national legislation. But not this time. The racial hostility in Philadelphia had prompted an unusually subdued response from federal officials in Washington, D.C.

After becoming president in 1963, Lyndon B. Johnson had worked with King on the fight for racial equality. The Voting Rights Act of 1965 served as the pinnacle achievement of their collaborative vision. But by 1966 new challenges had begun to complicate Johnson's presidency, especially the nation's ever increasing involvement in the civil war in Vietnam. Unrest was on the rise in the United States. Antiwar demonstrations. Race riots. Racial tensions.

All of these forces conspired against Johnson, and his push for civil rights began to falter. The expanding fight in Vietnam diverted funds away from the president's domestic goals, such as his desire to combat poverty. The year's civil rights bill was encountering resistance in Congress because some of its provisions—such as the elimination of laws that permitted housing discrimination—affected all Americans, not just Southerners, and many members of Congress had constituents who found the proposal threatening. The March Against Fear wasn't helping the president either. Instead of providing the public opinion lift that the previous year's walk from Selma had given to the Voting Rights Act of 1965, the march through Mississippi was alarming many Americans with news reports about cries for "black power."

The president had no patience for such calls. "We are not interested in black power, and we are not interested in white power," Johnson would tell members of the NAACP at their annual convention later that summer. "We are interested in American democratic power, with a small 'd.'" Militant cries for black power seemed no different to the president than the hateful calls of segregationists for white supremacy. Where was the compromise, he wondered. Where was the middle ground?

After Tuesday's visit to Philadelphia, King had complained to federal officials about the threatening reception they had received there, and he had asked for federal help with law enforcement during their return trip. Johnson had countered by inviting King, Carmichael, and others to the White House on Thursday to discuss their concerns. Movement leaders decided that such a trip would do more to undermine their momentum in Mississippi than to aid it, so they had declined the invitation. They wanted to stay with the marchers instead. That decision placed them in the midst of the attack in Canton instead of at the White House, where they otherwise would have been.

Martin Luther King, Jr., and other speakers used a bullhorn to amplify their voices when they returned to Philadelphia on June 24 in a demonstration of nonviolent courage.

So when leaders returned to Philadelphia on Friday, June 24, they did so without the protection of the national government. The president, instead of sending federal marshals or military personnel to the scene, had urged Mississippi's governor to beef up his own state security forces. Some felt that this communication had emboldened the governor to move forcefully against protesters in Canton. The fact that the president failed to criticize the Canton attack reinforced such thinking. Attorney General Nicholas Katzenbach, who served Johnson as the chief law enforcement officer in the land, didn't condemn the brutality in Canton either. As he saw it, the state troopers had encountered people who defied a local camping ban, not activists making a principled stand for equal justice.

King, Carmichael, and McKissick traveled from

Canton to Philadelphia with 15 carloads of supporters. They joined some 75 local blacks to form a procession of 300 marchers. Rows of state troopers lined the route of their planned march, which was less than reassuring to participants since these officers were members of the same force that had attacked protesters in Canton only the night before. *Could they be trusted? Whose side were they on?*

White onlookers vastly outnumbered the marchers, having flocked to Philadelphia from outlying areas to witness the new confrontation. This crowd of 2,000 was no more welcoming than the smaller one that had gathered three days earlier. According to CBS news announcer Harry Reasoner, Friday's "police protection was much better, but the jeering was worse" than it had been on Tuesday. Racial slurs flew through the air with the intensity of buckshot. So did soft drink bottles, eggs, and gobs of spit. A ribbon of rope and a single line of armed state troopers offered the only curtain of protection between demonstrators and this seething mass of rage.

All three leaders spoke at the courthouse, using a bullhorn in an attempt to make themselves heard above the unruly crowd. "We were brutalized here the other day," King observed, "and I guess someone felt that this would stop us and that we wouldn't come back. But we are right here today standing firm, saying we are going to have our freedom." After listening to brief speeches on the courthouse steps, marchers retraced their path. Partway back to the neighborhood where they'd started, a driver aimed his car into the crowd at such high speed that the marchers broke ranks and scattered for safety. James Lawson, who had traveled from Memphis to join the assembly, observed an officer plant himself in the path of the vehicle and force it to stop; then the driver and his passenger were arrested.

But other patrolmen, recalled Lawson, "turned their bayonets toward us."

“Can’t you see I’m a human being, just like you? Can’t you see it? Can’t you see it?”

Questions from a white woman targeted in the tear gas attack in Canton

“I couldn’t see it, friend, I couldn’t see it.”

Reply from a Canton policeman who participated in the attack

"The state of Mississippi could take no chance that the Negro may feel that change had come or may be just around the corner . . . [It] had to demonstrate that it was master."

James Meredith's explanation for the attack on marchers in Canton on June 23, 1966

By the time James Meredith returned to his walk on June 25, the objective of one man had become a goal for thousands. Meredith (center, with, from left, Martin Luther King, Jr., and Floyd McKissick) reached Tougaloo

CHAPTER 9

REUNITED

ND THEN JAMES MEREDITH WAS BACK.

He rejoined the march on Friday, June 24, the day after the brutal tear gas attack in Canton and the same day movement leaders revisited Philadelphia. More than two weeks had passed since his shooting, and Meredith had become an abstract motivation for the protest. He had had no interest in returning to the march while it diverted into the delta, but now that participants were back on course—his course, down Highway 51—Meredith was ready to reassert his place as a marcher, indeed, as the marcher-in-chief. Although organizers had known he could return at any time, they still struggled to incorporate yet another force into the dynamic of their complicated endeavor.

Things didn't go well at first.

That morning, while Meredith was traveling toward Canton and representatives of the march were revisiting Philadelphia, the rest of the participants in the march had remained in Canton to promote the walk's final voter registration drive. By the time the Philadelphia contingent returned to Canton, their fellow activists had completed their demonstration at the local courthouse and begun marching south on Highway 51. Sunday's march into Jackson would depart from Tougaloo College, an historic black institution about 18 miles south of Canton and 8 miles

DATES WALKED: June 24–25 **MILES WALKED:** 37 **ROUTE:** Canton to Tougaloo College, Tougaloo

north of downtown Jackson. Organizers had planned to spread the hike to Tougaloo over Friday and Saturday, but when a troop of 45 seasoned walkers got going, they pushed on all the way.

This accomplishment displeased Meredith because it had been his intention to cover the highway beyond Canton himself. He'd planned to walk those miles originally, and, now that he was back, he felt robbed of the chance to walk them still. Everything seemed to have changed during his absence. The walk to Jackson—his walk to Jackson—had morphed into something far different from his original vision. Women and children were everywhere. The operation had ballooned in scale yet lacked the military precision he would have demanded. And his own homecoming felt preempted by the perseverance of the other walkers. Drawing on his capacity for independence, Meredith announced plans to hike from Canton to Tougaloo anyway the next day. If folks wanted to join him, they could. Meanwhile, he traveled with his mother to Tougaloo College, where they were to stay as guests of the campus dean.

Meredith had arrived in Canton with his mother and a small group of supporters at about the same time that movement leaders returned from Philadelphia. All soon learned about the march's latest housing crisis. Organizers had planned originally to spend two nights in Canton, and even though their attempt to camp there the previous night had led them to be teargassed and beaten, they still hoped to prevail. Surely the severity of the attack would embarrass city officials and force them to meet their demands. But condemnation was muted, in part because of a general decline in public sympathy due to the walk's "black power" phrase, but probably also because the Canton attack had taken place after dark, making it difficult for journalists to convey the full horror of the scene. Despite a series of meetings, Canton city officials refused to reverse their prohibition. Meredith caught one of the day's debates and wasn't impressed. "I don't know what's happening over there," he told reporters after attending a meeting of local black leaders and march organizers. "I think something is wrong. The whole damn thing smells to me."

The results of the day's negotiations proved disappointing to many activists: Marchers got permission to hold a meeting on school property, but not to camp there. Some saw this arrangement as an outright betrayal of the movement's commitment to nonviolent protest. Since when did the movement tolerate discrimination? Shouldn't marchers just try to camp again anyway, with or without permission? Leaders in the local black community advocated for less confrontation; they still needed to be able to work with white officials after the march moved on. Representatives of SNCC and CORE were willing to force another showdown, but Martin Luther King, Jr., counseled restraint. In the end they chose to focus on reaching Jackson rather than on diverting their resources yet again. Still, people grumbled.

Farm laborers paused from weeding cotton to wave at marchers hiking from Canton to Tougaloo on June 24.

In the end, even the compromise to use the grounds for a rally proved meaningless. When a crowd of more than 1,000 converged on the ball field where they'd been attacked the previous night, they discovered that local officials had soaked it with water from a fire hydrant, turning their rallying point into a muddy mess. This defeat hit hard as marchers made do once again with makeshift sleeping arrangements at local churches.

When Meredith returned to Canton on Saturday, June 25, to begin walking toward Tougaloo, law enforcement officers refused at first to serve as his escort. They'd already covered those same miles the day before, and they didn't feel obliged to do so again. Eventually, Madison County Sheriff Jack Cauthen agreed to protect Meredith for a symbolic two-mile hike out of Canton. Meredith accepted his offer and set off in the company of his traveling companions and 126 veterans of the March Against Fear. Once again Meredith wore his trademark pith helmet and carried the African walking stick that he'd gripped in his hand 19 days earlier during his shooting.

When he reached the end of the sheriff's jurisdiction, Officer Charles Snodgrass, the head of the Mississippi highway patrol, offered to provide security en route to Tougaloo after all if Meredith gave the right answer to one question: "Are you armed?" Snodgrass knew Meredith had been threatening to return to Mississippi with a gun, and he didn't like that idea. Meredith raised his arms in reply, allowing the officer to pat him down and confirm that he carried no weapons. Prior to his return to Mississippi, Meredith told reporters, Snodgrass had assured him that his deputies would protect him. "He has given me his word," said Meredith, and so Meredith had felt no need to arm himself in self-defense.

It was Meredith's 33rd birthday, and he started out strong as he left Canton. More marchers joined the procession, dropped off by cars heading south toward their overnight stop at Tougaloo. Soon the assembly swelled to 200, then to some 300 marchers. The lingering effects of his wounds may well have contributed to Meredith's periodic irritability. Twice when representatives from King's SCLC approached him, he shoved them aside. No one was quite sure why. When he began to limp, Meredith traveled part of the remaining distance in a car, then waited and rejoined the march. King,

Meredith required medical attention during his walk from Canton to Tougaloo on June 25. He continued to be bothered by lingering effects from his shooting near Hernando 19 days earlier.

ever the peacemaker, organized a sizable contingent to head north from Tougaloo as a sort of greeting committee. The two groups of walkers met and then merged, swelling to a crowd of nearly 1,000 participants.

King and Meredith, walking side by side, looked behind them as the throng reached the Tougaloo campus. "I hope this is in light of what you wanted," King said to Meredith, who, his mood improving, had thrown an arm over King's shoulder.

"This is the most beautiful thing I have seen in a long time," Meredith replied.

All day thousands of supporters streamed toward Tougaloo College. As many as 10,000 arrived, in fact, drawn by a star-studded rally set to occur on campus that night, the eve of what organizers hoped would be a triumphant march into Jackson the next day. Logistical planning for the march had shifted weeks earlier from James Lawson's church in Memphis to Pratt Memorial United Methodist Church in Jackson. In addition to coordinating the care for and transportation of participants in the march, staffers from the sponsoring organizations promoted its finale, too, a rally that would take place on the grounds of the state capitol in Jackson. "Everyone is invited," proclaimed their announcement to supporters. Or at least everyone who respected "the basic philosophy of nonviolence."

The evening program at Tougaloo College strayed from the speeches and freedom songs that had been the norm during the march. This time Hollywood celebrities took the stage. Noted black entertainer Sammy Davis, Jr., performed. Movie stars Marlon Brando and Burt Lancaster stepped out to praise the marchers. Comedian Dick Gregory, a longtime ally of Meredith's who had walked on his behalf the day after his shooting, cracked jokes for the audience. He poked fun at both the South and the "black power" phrase. "When y'all get to saying it down here, it sounds like you're saying 'Black Powder'!"

Legendary soul man James Brown was on hand with his band to perform the closing act of Saturday's show. Although the usual evening planning meeting had kept movement organizers from attending the beginning of the rally, King and Stokely Carmichael excused themselves early when they heard the popular musician begin to sing. They didn't want to miss his act and headed to the concert together.

King said, as he departed, "I'm sorry, y'all. James Brown is on. I'm gone."

“We are not going to stay ignorant, and backward, and scared.”

Annie Devine, Canton resident and Mississippi activist

“Aren’t we civilized enough to ignore these rabble rousers?”

Mary Rose, complaining about the attention being paid to marchers in Mississippi

"Sing a song full of the faith that the dark past has taught us; Sing a song full of the hope that the present has brought us; Facing the rising sun of our new day begun, Let us march on till victory is won."

Rhythm and blues vocalist Maybelle Smith at the rally in Jackson, singing a verse of "Lift Every Voice and Sing," which has been called the Negro national anthem

Marchers and supporters massed on the grounds of the Mississippi State Capitol in Jackson on Sunday, June 26, for the closing rally of the March Against Fear. CBS aired a

CHAPTER 10

FINALE

HE NEXT MORNING, Sunday, June 26, about 2,000 participants set off from Tougaloo College bound for the state capitol in downtown Jackson. "We've got the light of freedom," they sang as the final day's walk got under way. Compared to recent hikes, this one was practically a stroll. The marchers departed at 11 a.m., and they only needed to cover eight miles by late afternoon. Organizers knew the procession would swell in size as it advanced through Jackson en route to their final rallying point, and planners had established eight additional departure points around the city that would intersect at designated spots with the main corps.

As anticipated, thousands of Jacksonians joined the march, some by design, others irresistibly drawn from their porches. Overwhelmingly they were black. Maids and farm workers. Students and day laborers. Young and old. At one point a local brass band added its voice to the parade, and such songs as "When the Saints Go Marching In" became part of an ongoing soundtrack of marching feet, singing, and the shouting of slogans.

Thousands of additional participants were on hand, too, having traveled to Jackson by chartered planes and buses specifically in support of the march. Labor leader Walter Reuther, accompanied by his wife, had journeyed from Chicago with 10 buses full of union supporters. Martin Luther King, Jr., was joined by his wife, Coretta, and their three oldest

DATE WALKED: June 26 **MILES WALKED:** 8 **ROUTE:** Tougaloo College, Tougaloo, to Jackson

children. Members of James Meredith's family stayed at home in New York, which was not surprising given his dislike of including women and children in potentially dangerous protests. Whitney Young of the National Urban League surprised event organizers by reversing his earlier rejection of the march; his group would help sponsor it after all, and he, too, traveled to Jackson for the finale.

Mindful of the weather—it would be another humid day with 90-plus-degree temperatures—many participants came attired in short-sleeved shirts, protective hats, and sunglasses. Meredith wore his pith helmet, Stokely Carmichael his bib overalls. Entertainers from the previous night's gala mingled and walked with the crowd. Not everyone hiked all eight miles, Meredith included. As always cars helped ferry people toward the finish line, and the hot weather proved as challenging as the distance for many.

In an era before convenience stores dotted the urban landscape, marchers sought all available sources for hydration. They drained the supplies of soft drink machines that they passed. They accepted cups of water and lemonade from residents along their path. One SCLC staffer purchased a solid block of ice and smashed the five-pound mass into smaller pieces that could be wrapped into makeshift cold packs and nestled on the backs of necks.

Several layers of security protected marchers. As was typical for such a large event, organizers designated dozens of marshals to accompany the walkers and reinforce their commitment to order and nonviolence. One hundred representatives of the Deacons for Defense and Justice mingled in the throng, too. In addition to them, hundreds of state and local law enforcement representatives guarded the route and beyond—including a handful of the black policemen who recently had begun to integrate Jackson's police force.

Although officers were assigned to protect marchers, that didn't ensure that they brought respect to the task. "Goddamn you, nigger, move that truck or I'll blow your goddamn head off," a white police officer barked at the SCLC's Robert Green, even though the chief of police had given him permission to drive the ambulance truck alongside the march.

"Shoot! Shoot!" cheered white onlookers.

During the final rally in Jackson on June 26, the speakers' platform (visible at the bottom of this aerial view) faced the Mississippi State Capitol. Law enforcement personnel formed a security buffer behind the crowd.

Law enforcement was on hand to defend local territory from approaching marchers, too. A chain of soldiers from the state's National Guard helped to surround the grounds at the state capitol, barring access to the south side of the structure, which was home to a revered Civil War memorial to the women of the Confederacy—the mothers and daughters, the wives and sisters of Confederate soldiers. Participants could only rally at the reverse side of the building, the symbolism of which did not go unnoticed by citizens who until recently had routinely been required to use inferior entrances to public spaces. Still, organizers made the best of it, relieved to have gained permission to rally anywhere on the public grounds.

It was approaching 4 p.m. when the procession neared the state capitol. Three weeks earlier to the day, Meredith had embarked on a journey from Memphis to Jackson. Now, a goal set by one man was being completed by 15,000 people. "Bring those folks who have been doing most of the walking up front here," suggested Carmichael as they neared their destination. The front row of a march was a coveted spot, reserved for leaders and celebrity guests. Carmichael wanted to recognize everyday folks, too, those who had worn out their shoes, slept on hard ground night after night, and sweated through Mississippi heat day after day.

People of all ages witnessed the rally in Jackson on June 26, including young people who would be in their 50s and 60s today.

Local blacks weren't the only ones who turned out for the march and rally. Thousands of whites did, too, swelling the crowd to 20,000 or more, although few of them were on hand to support the cause of civil rights. Some downtown businesses closed for the day rather than serve the integrated crowd. Many white onlookers brandished the Confederate battle flag, jeering, name-calling, and spitting at participants in the procession.

Marchers waved flags, too. In addition to carrying tiny U.S. flags, people paraded with banners of purple, green, and red that read: MEREDITH MISSISSIPPI MARCH. They held signs, too, with slogans ranging from militant,

"BLACK POWER BY ANY MEANS NECESSARY," to catchy, "MOVE ON OVER—OR WE'LL MOVE ON OVER YOU," to traditional, "FREEDOM NOW," and hybrid, "FREEDOM IS BLACK POWER." There were even bumper stickers, courtesy of SNCC, which representatives were happy to slap on any available surface, even police cars: "WE'RE THE GREATEST."

"This little light of mine, I'm gonna let it shine," sang some marchers as they approached the end of their journey. In many ways, just getting to Jackson was accomplishment enough, but the ending of such a long endeavor called for a commemoration, and, after the throng had settled on the capitol grounds, a two-hour program of speeches, songs, and prayers commenced. Presenters appeared on a makeshift stage with a sound system inadequate for the enormous crowd. News helicopters hovering overhead made it that much harder for the audience to hear, but folks persevered, as they'd been doing for weeks.

When it was Meredith's turn to speak, he proclaimed that "the system of white supremacy will reign no longer." White rule depended on breeding a culture of fear among blacks, he said, and the cycle had to be broken. He concluded with a gracious acknowledgment for all the efforts that had assured the completion of his walk. "I want to thank all of the people who took up the march," he said. "I want to thank the women who stood by the road with ice in the buckets." He continued, "I want to thank the leaders who took up this most difficult task, who faced the bricks and ax handles in Philadelphia, who looked murderers in the face." He recognized the people who had endured the attack in Canton, too, and then concluded, "I thank you all." The crowd roared in approval and tribute.

Carmichael followed Meredith to the stage: "We have to stop being ashamed of being black!" he urged the crowd. "We have to move to a position where we can feel strength and unity amongst each other from Watts to Harlem, where we won't ever be afraid!" Although he didn't use the phrase "black power," he certainly described it, and in defiant terms. Blacks "must build a power base so strong in this country that it will bring them to their knees every time they mess with us!" When Floyd McKissick took the stage to represent CORE, he tried to defuse the fuss over black power. "It's just an adjective inserted before a noun," he reminded listeners.

As always, King appeared last. Three summers before he had spoken at the Lincoln Memorial during the March on Washington about his dream for the country. Now—after the bombing that killed four girls in Birmingham, after the murders of three civil rights workers outside Philadelphia, after the confrontation on the Edmund Pettus Bridge in Selma, after the tear-gassing of marchers in Canton over the pitching of some tents—after all those struggles and more, his sunny vision from 1963 seemed more dream-like than ever.

True, advocates for racial justice had made progress, especially with the passage of the Voting Rights Act in 1965, but so many challenges remained.

Racism and prejudice.

The trap of poverty.

Enduring segregation.

But King still had hope. He still reached for the future as he spoke in Jackson. A better day would come, he insisted. A better day that didn't require the confrontational tone of black power.

"This will be the day of all men living together as brothers. It will not be the day of the white man. It will not be the day of the black man," he said.

"It will be the day of man *as* man!"

"If my daddy had done this,
it would have been a lot better for me.
Now all of this ain't going to help me none—
it's too late for that—but I'm doing it
for the children."

Monroe Williams, age 78, on June 26, 1966, while walking with
his cane to the state capitol in his first demonstration

"I urge all of our citizens to ignore
the end of this small storm
and to keep their eyes and their efforts
on the peaceful and prosperous future
that we are building together
in this great state."

Mississippi Governor Paul Johnson during
the final weekend of the march

"You who live in the North: Do not think that Mississippi has no relevance to you . . . my Mississippi is everywhere. And the hour is getting late."

James Meredith, writing about the March Against Fear for the *Saturday Evening Post,* August 13, 1966

Black and white children played together in Grenada on September 14, offering a stark contrast to two days earlier when local whites attacked black students after schools were forced to integrate.

CHAPTER 11

AFTERSHOCKS

HE MARCH AGAINST FEAR stands as one of the greatest protests of the civil rights era. By the time participants reached Jackson, a fluid combination of countless volunteers had walked for 305 miles on a route connecting Memphis to the Mississippi state capital. This effort dwarfed the scale of the previous year's march from Selma to Montgomery in Alabama. The campaign through Mississippi lasted more than four times as long (22 days compared with 5) and hikers traveled nearly six times farther (54 miles were covered in 1965). In Alabama, they'd camped 4 nights; marchers in Mississippi spent 16 nights sleeping en route, never staying more than twice in any one spot. Organizers and volunteers fed some version of three meals a day to an ever changing number of people for 20 days straight.

By such measures, it would seem the march should have been championed as a success. Participants had, after all, reached Jackson. Fifteen thousand people celebrated this accomplishment by joining the final capitol rally. The three-week-long effort resulted in just over 4,000 black Mississippians registering to vote, and inspired countless others to do so later on. March organizers had depended on the kindness of strangers, the whims of the weather, and their confidence that people would show up—and it had worked.

Or had it?

No one knew it at the time, but the campaign through Mississippi wasn't just one of the most ambitious marches of the civil rights era; it was the last great march of the period. Even before undertaking it, Martin Luther King, Jr., had recognized that the formula for securing equality was shifting. Convincing the federal government to enforce without bias the laws that already protected white citizens had taken years of courage and hard work. It would be even tougher to persuade ordinary citizens that African Americans deserved the same opportunities that white people took for granted, from comfortable housing to the benefits of inherited wealth.

The civil rights movement paid a heavy price for undertaking the March Against Fear. For starters, the endeavor cost far more than organizers were able to raise for its support. Civil rights groups, most notably King's SCLC, had to close a fund-raising gap of $20,000, a sum equivalent to about $150,000 today. Even worse, despite the completion of the march, the civil rights bill of 1966 died in the U.S. Senate three months after the march, torpedoed in part by the negative press about cries for "black power." Elements of the bill's fair housing provision made it into the decade's final civil rights act in 1968, the Fair Housing Act, but the era of sweeping civil rights legislation was over.

Perhaps the most costly effect of the march, though, was the discord it created within and between the various civil rights organizations. Never again would movement leaders undertake such a collaborative venture. The unity of the civil rights movement began to fray. Tensions that surfaced during the walk—over the merits of nonviolence, over black power, over the role of white allies—persisted after it ended. The movement would never be the same.

Many white activists stepped back after the protest in Mississippi. "We listened to what SNCC was saying," recalled college student David Dawley, "and there was a sense that this was a time when blacks had the right to define the movement and that blacks would lead the strategy." He added: "I accepted that strategy. My friends accepted that strategy. So we moved on to work with whites on issues that we felt we should work with. In the next year that was not civil rights, that was Vietnam." But SNCC, instead of being reinvigorated by focusing on black power, foundered, and by 1970 the organization was gone. Stokely Carmichael had moved to Africa by then to support the freedom struggles of that continent's blacks. Later he

Smoldering fires and the shells of burned-out buildings attested to the destructive force of two nights of rioting in the African-American section of Cleveland, Ohio, during mid-July 1966.

changed his name to Kwame Ture, in honor of two African political leaders.

The news media continued to focus more on black power than on the legacy of the march itself. Or rather, black power seemed to become its legacy. When national journalists departed from Mississippi, they left behind its examples of poverty and oppression and began covering the growing unrest in the nation's urban centers instead. Riots and protests broke out that summer in more than 20 cities, including Minneapolis, Baltimore, Omaha, Los Angeles, Atlanta, and Cleveland. Journalists sought to connect this violence to Stokely Carmichael's cries for black power. But Carmichael hadn't provoked the riots; he had merely named a frustration that fed the powerlessness and unrest of people trapped by racism and poverty because of the color of their skin.

The riots offered obvious evidence of rage, but few journalists dug through the rubble to uncover their root causes: lack of employment, jobs that didn't pay a living wage, neglected housing stock, limited access to health care, inferior schools, lack of mobility out of neighborhoods that had turned into ghettos, and more. People whose ancestors had been enslaved by chains and brute force found themselves trapped, too, trapped in a cycle of poverty from which it was virtually impossible to escape.

"It is necessary to understand that Black Power is a cry of disappointment," especially among young people, wrote King the year after the march. "For 12 years I, and others like me, had held out radiant promises of progress. I had preached to them about my dream . . . I had urged them to have faith in America and white society. Their hopes had soared . . . They were now hostile because they were watching the dream that they had so readily accepted turn into a frustrating nightmare."

Following the march through Mississippi, a group known as the Black Panthers became the most visible advocates for black power. This grassroots network of mostly young, mostly urban individuals cared less about the lofty ideals of nonviolence and dreams of a beloved community than about the need to achieve more immediate gains. Breakfast for impoverished black schoolchildren. Neighborhood centers for free health care. Protection for minorities from racially motivated acts of police brutality.

Stokely Carmichael (at microphone with arm raised) spoke at a 1968 rally in Oakland, California, on behalf of jailed Black Panther co-founder Huey Newton.

Children flocked to welcome James Meredith (visible behind the children, wearing necktie) to a summer festival in the Watts neighborhood of Los Angeles, California, on August 12, 1966, one year after deadly riots had caused millions of dollars of damage.

But the Black Panthers' assertiveness, especially their insistence on their right to armed self-defense, drew more notice than their efforts to effect change. Such boldness only reinforced white worries over the idea of black power. No matter how hard advocates for racial empowerment tried to reassure whites that black power didn't mean black violence, those concerns remained, and this disconnect became one more excuse for whites to ignore the impact of racial inequality.

The year after the March Against Fear, James Meredith returned to Mississippi to resume hiking. Meredith didn't like to leave a job unfinished. He went back to the site of his shooting and walked for 11 days, traveling from there to Canton along Highway 51. "I had to continue," he explained, "to be sure that I was not afraid." In subsequent years, he has undertaken other cause-inspired walks. One thousand miles in 1969 from Illinois to New York in support of African-American community organizations. Forty-some miles across Mississippi in 1974 to encourage others to walk as far as their courthouses and register to vote. Repeating his walk from Memphis to Jackson at age 62 on its 30th anniversary to support literacy and public libraries.

Although Meredith mounted political campaigns on several occasions, he never ran for governor of Mississippi, and he has never won elected office. His most controversial act was to align himself later in life with the Republican Party and some of its most conservative figures, including those seen as opponents of racial equality. He remains fiercely independent, proud of his contributions to history, loyal to Ole Miss and the state of his birth, the place that he calls home.

"'Mississippi' is the most powerful word in the English language," he observed in 2012, because he believes the state's name evokes all manner of meanings and associations for anyone who hears the word.

Aubrey Norvell, the man arrested for shooting Meredith, has never explained his actions. When he appeared in court on November 21, 1966, he surprised many by pleading guilty to assault and battery with intent to kill. By doing so, he escaped trial, and, as a result, escaped formal questioning about his motives. The presiding judge sentenced Norvell to two years in Mississippi's Parchman Penitentiary, the same place Carmichael and other Freedom Riders had staged hunger strikes five years earlier. Norvell became eligible for parole 18 months later and was released soon after.

Conspiracy theories about the shooting continued to appear, including ones that claimed Meredith had never been wounded at all, despite the fact that countless tiny bumps of bird shot remain buried below the surface of his skin. Madison County Sheriff Jack Cauthen, who had touched Meredith's back as the two of them discussed security for his walk toward Tougaloo in 1966, later claimed that "there hadn't been no pellets or shots in James's back . . . I don't think he was shot, no sir." That same willingness to ignore historical fact emboldened some white citizens in Canton to misremember the June 23 attack in their city as an incident of drive-by harassment during which whites shot off firecrackers. "There actually never was any bloodshed or anything like that here during that time," a local news reporter would claim during a 1982 interview.

Indeed, the entire March Against Fear became one of those moments in history that most people, black and white, seemed to want to forget. Few have recalled or celebrated it. Those too young to remember that era have rarely heard of it. Reasons for this historical amnesia are plentiful. Perhaps because it lacks the uplift and stirring accomplishment of the previous year's trek from Selma. Or because it defies the tidy narrative that portrays the civil rights movement as one great push toward progress, stopped only by King's assassination. Or because it exposed wounds from the legacy of slavery that white folks just weren't ready to face. It was far easier to let the endeavor fade from recollection than to face its uncomfortable legacy.

Ignoring the past doesn't mean it didn't take place, though, any more than pretending Meredith doesn't have bird shot embedded beneath his skin can erase the fact that he was shot. It happened. For better or worse, the marchers reached Jackson. But the conversation that Meredith tried to start about race was never completed, and the aftershocks of that unfinished business have sent tremors through the nation ever since. It is not hard to hear the echoes of an earlier era's calls for empowerment in today's cries about an old, old concern.

That black lives matter.

The pace of social change isn't a steady, upward slope. Progress comes in bursts. Change doesn't occur because it should happen. Change takes place because people push for it to happen. There will always be forces that resist change, if for no other reason than change can make people afraid, and, as the March Against Fear showed, when people are afraid, they can become loud and violent opponents. But over the course of human history, as in the course of American history, the forces of change eventually prevail.

Such struggles are not for the faint of heart. Nor are they for the impatient. Change takes time, sometimes a lifetime, sometimes more than one lifetime. At its best, the commitment to bring about change can become a pursuit akin to the quest King and others undertook to create a beloved community. Some may find themselves invested in the journey as part of a lifelong connection to the best potential of the human spirit. Others may take part in punctuated moments of activism, whether an attempt to walk from Memphis to Jackson in 1966 or an effort to assure that black lives do matter in the 21st century.

Change doesn't happen without setbacks, either. Gains that seem permanent can erode. The Voting Rights Act of 1965 stands as the perfect example of hard-fought rights undermined decades later. In 2013, a case reached the U.S. Supreme Court that led to the nullifying of key parts of the Voting Rights Act. This ruling permitted subsequent legislation by many states to impose new restrictions on the voting process for millions of citizens. But fresh quests for progress tend to follow such losses, and legal challenges to these restrictive voting rules are ongoing.

Similarly, in 2015, the Confederate battle flag was so broadly condemned as a toxic totem of racism that it became harder to defend it as merely a symbol of reverence for past valor. Flags came down from many public spaces and dropped out of sight from major retail stores. Voices questioned, as well, the continued appropriateness of commemorative memorials to a lost war of rebellion, setting off a debate likely to continue for some time. Removing every monument to the Civil War won't erase the effects of slavery, but matching them with monuments to the history of slavery, the victims of lynchings, and the advocates for justice from the civil rights movement might help.

"Only a refusal to hate or kill can put an end to the chain of violence in the world and lead us toward a community where men can live together without fear," King wrote soon after the March Against Fear. "Our goal is to create a beloved community and this will require a qualitative change in our souls as well as a quantitative change in our lives."

What did King mean? To make a qualitative change, King was asking people to search their hearts and root out hatreds and prejudices. They'd have to face their fears. The quantitative change that King sought was for all the members of American society to address the legacy of slavery. Not until an inheritance of social and economic progress replaced an inheritance of poverty would the nation truly be able to heal and move on.

This work remains unfinished.

And so the march continues.

The march toward equality. The quest for social justice. The push to bring out the best instincts in the human family, rather than its worst.

The determination to diminish the power of fear.

“I’m convinced that Mississippi will never be the same again.”

Martin Luther King, Jr., following the visit to Grenada, Mississippi, by the March Against Fear

“After they leave, everything will be the same again.”

Sheriff’s deputy, regarding the visit to Grenada, Mississippi, by the March Against Fear

AUTHOR'S NOTE

ALTHOUGH I'VE SPENT my adult life in the Midwest, my roots are decidedly southern. I was born in Tennessee and raised in Virginia during the era of the civil rights movement. Perhaps I've been drawn to explore history from that time, from that region, because I've wanted to make myself whole, to close the gap in understanding between the world that I saw as a child and the world as it really was.

It was a big gap.

I have a wisp of a childhood recollection that serves as a testament to that chasm. In the memory fragment, I'm riding through the Deep South during the 1960s along the usual backcountry roads of the day. Me, my mother, and her mother. The drive from our home in Virginia to my grandmother's house in Louisiana would have taken days, but I remember no more than 30 minutes of the trip.

My memory takes form as we pull into a gas station in the middle of nowhere, nestled into a random T-intersection. It's a simple place. Maybe two pumps. Maybe one service bay. Rough woods line the road. Nothing else keeps it company. The lone attendant is white, like us. He understands why the adults have decided to stop: Marchers are coming. Yes, we can wait with him while they pass. Then he locks the station doors.

We don't wait long. A group of people walks into view. Perhaps 40, as my adult mind looks back in time to count them. Who knows, though? I was just a little kid, and it all happened so long ago. The people amble past, keeping their distance, seeming not to see our shelter, never crossing the road toward us. I watch, baffled, not quite sure why this troop aroused concern. They're just people walking with quiet purpose toward some unknown destination. People separated from me by a thin plate of glass, hardly a worthy defense if one were needed.

In two, maybe three minutes, they're gone. The grown-ups around me relax. We thank the attendant, return to our car, and continue our drive. Our destination lies somewhere toward the direction from which the marchers came, and that's where my recollection ends. I've forgotten the rest of the trip. All that remains is a memory of people around me feeling afraid.

This sensory fragment is one of many that transport me through time and space to my southern childhood. I grew up in Lexington, Virginia, a town that seemed to have cornered the market on Civil War–era history. Two academic institutions anchored the community: Virginia Military Institute, whose early students had fought for the Confederacy, and Washington and Lee University, which had renamed itself to honor its postwar president, Confederate general Robert E. Lee. Monuments to the Civil War populated the landscape.

I found the stories of my town enshrined in the pages of my Virginia state history books, a subject we studied throughout both fourth and seventh grades. These textbook accounts of the Civil War era were written with a compelling narrative of valor and honor, of compassion and decency. A narrative of noble purpose and stolen opportunities. A narrative that, many years later, I would realize had a special name: the Lost Cause.

My family was one of the more progressive ones in this small community. When local schools finally had no choice but to integrate, my parents ignored the advice of their peers: Just put in a request for Ann to have a white teacher, they had suggested; that way she'll stay in a white classroom. It was the summer of 1966—the summer of my memory of finding fear along the highways of Mississippi during the March Against Fear—and such a system didn't sound like integration to my parents. As a result, I was one of a handful of white children placed into a classroom of color, led by veteran educator Christine Warren, a wonderful teacher to whom I dedicated an earlier book, *Marching to the Mountaintop*.

I've thought more about fourth grade while writing this book than in all the intervening decades. I enjoyed my year with Mrs. Warren. She turned me into a reader. She inspired me to start a stamp collection. She cemented my love of history. I look back at the year we spent together and marvel at the grit it must have taken for this proud, bright woman to teach an historical narrative that excused the enslavement of her ancestors and that made it noble to have fought for the perpetuation of slavery.

I left behind the South of my childhood when I chose to enroll at Beloit College in Wisconsin in 1975, and I've only returned as a visitor since. By moving away, I gained the perspective that comes with distance. By living through the subsequent decades, I've gained the perspective that comes through time and experience. Looking back, the manipulation all seems so easy. The compelling narrative of a Lost Cause that left whites supreme. The perpetuation of systems that kept whites in control. The reinforcement that monuments gave to an account of history which focused on the glories of white manhood to the exclusion of almost everything else.

Maybe that's why I've spent the past 15 years writing about social justice history—to fill in those gaps. Maybe that's why it literally does take generations to bring about social change. How many of my southern peers, raised on the narrative of the Lost Cause, ever learned a corrective accounting for our past? How often have we perpetuated the lies taught to us without knowing we ourselves were taught lies?

When I settled in the Midwest two years after finishing college, I took up residence within a few miles of U.S. Highway 51. That same asphalt ribbon that Meredith sought to follow from Memphis to Jackson cuts a path near the four homes I've made for myself over the past four decades. Perhaps that pavement has called to me in its own quiet way for years, the way roads can lure you to travel just a bit farther to look around a bend, and then the next bend, and so on, until you've crossed a county line or entered a new state. By living within a mile or two of Highway 51, I could, at any time, point myself toward Illinois, head south, and travel back in time.

And I have done so repeatedly during the past dozen years.

Lessons well taught can be hard to unlearn. Lessons learned in childhood almost become embedded in our DNA. Until our personal experiences intersect with alternative points of view, our opinions can seem as set in stone as the statues that towered over my childhood. Removing the Confederate battle flag and the most offending monuments doesn't automatically erase the thoughts in people's heads. It takes time to do that. Time and encounters with realities that make a lie of old lessons. Time and the experiences of traveling into new territories.

Thank you, dear reader, for sharing this journey with me through time and space, around wooded corners and toward distant horizons. May we keep following pathways that take us toward a richer understanding of the human family, toward a greater sense of community.

May we keep following the tramp, tramp, tramp of marching feet.

ACKNOWLEDGMENTS

IT TAKES MANY HANDS TO MAKE A BOOK. This one could not have come into being without the staff and resources of several key archives, especially at the University of Memphis, where members of the Preservation and Special Collections Department invariably serve with professionalism and grace. Many thanks to Christopher Michael Ratliff, who prepared scans of key images, and who, along with colleagues Sharon Banker, Brigitte Billeadeaux, and James Cushing, provided tireless access to collections during multiple research trips.

I also visited the University of Mississippi's Archives and Special Collections in Oxford, where I was able to immerse myself in the papers of James Meredith; the Mississippi Department of Archives and History in Jackson, where I viewed local print news and video footage from the events of 1966; and the Paley Center for Media in New York City, which allowed me to watch and transcribe the CBS special report from 1966, "The March in Mississippi." Online collections added to my understanding and enriched the visual presentation of this book, as well, most notably the Jim Peppler *Southern Courier* Photograph Collection at the Alabama Department of Archives and History and the Bob Fitch Photography Archive at the Stanford University Libraries.

Peppler, Fitch, and other photographers covered the distance from Memphis to Jackson under all manner of circumstances to record the March Against Fear. Their work, undertaken tirelessly and in difficult—and often dangerous circumstances—is one of the unsung labors of democracy. Photojournalists record the first draft of history, one that preserves an intimate and immediate connection back through time. I am grateful to have been able to draw from these archives and other sources to better understand the period for the illustration of this book.

It was my privilege to interview two very special figures from the era during my research, starting with James Lawson, an essential figure in the civil rights movement whose contributions are all too often overlooked. I am grateful to James Meredith, both for making history during his lifetime and for graciously sharing his reflections about it when we visited in Jackson during 2012. I've drawn on the memories of other eyewitnesses, too, including march participant Stanley Plona, who somehow not only found time to keep a written diary of his experiences but, some years later, managed to have it added to the archives at the University of Memphis.

Historian and author Aram Goudsouzian, whose *Down to the Crossroads* stands as the definitive account of the March Against Fear, encouraged my interest in this history from the get-go and has remained supportive of my effort to share it with young people, including by serving as an expert reader for the project during this book's production. I am likewise indebted to Frank Roberts of New York University for his careful review of this text.

Infinite thanks, as always, must go to my allies at National Geographic, starting with the book's in-house editorial team, including project editor Becky Baines, her boss, Erica Green, and her boss, Jennifer Emmett, my guiding editor on 10 titles with this publisher. Quite fortuitously, this editorial triumvirate added Catherine Frank to the project team, and Catherine contributed her expert guidance to the creative process of perfecting the book. It has been a joy to collaborate with them all.

Other essential players in the production process included Michaela Weglinski, Grace Hill, Lori Epstein, and Jim Hiscott, who created the book's stunning cover and design. Many thanks to Ruth Chamblee, Laurie Hembree, and the entire sales and marketing team, as well. Beyond National Geographic, I owe thanks to Samantha Poyer who, as an intern from Beloit College, offered invaluable assistance during my research process, and whose camaraderie was inspiring during what is otherwise such a solitary experience.

As always, I am indebted to members of my critique group, who keep making me a better writer; to friends near and far; to my grown sons, who inspired me to become an author and inspire me still; and to my brother and his wife, essential souls on life's journey. My parents, who have lived to reach historic ages, have contributed in countless ways to my love of story, including by putting me on a path that intersected with history during the March Against Fear so long ago.

My gratitude is as endless as the unspooling pavement of an inviting roadway.

BIBLIOGRAPHY

"19 Named in New Indictment in 3 Mississippi Rights Killings." *New York Times*, March 1, 1967.

"Apology Made for Meredith Death Report." *Editor & Publisher*, June 11, 1966.

"Arrest 3 Marchers Then Open Up Park." *Jackson Clarion-Ledger*, June 17, 1966.

Barrett, Russell. "Roads and Ruts in Mississippi." Speech Delivered at Rust College, Holly Springs, Mississippi, February 1, 1966. Russell H. Barrett Collection. University of Mississippi, Department of Archives and Special Collections.

Branch, Taylor. *At Canaan's Edge: America in the King Years 1965–68*. New York: Simon & Schuster, 2006.

———. *Parting the Waters: America in the King Years 1954–63*. New York: Simon & Schuster, 1988.

Branson, Reed. "Meredith to Follow 1966 Path in Crusade." Memphis *Commercial Appeal*, undated, 1996.

Burks, Edward C. "Meredith Begins Vote March Today." *New York Times*, June 5, 1966.

Carmichael, Stokely. "What We Want." *New York Review of Books*. September 22, 1966.

Carson, Clayborne, and David J. Garrow. *The Eyes on the Prize Civil Rights Reader: Documents, Speeches, and Firsthand Accounts from the Black Freedom Struggle*. New York: Penguin Books, 1991.

Citizen King. A ROJA Productions Film for *American Experience*. WGBH Educational Foundation, 2004. Transcript available online.

"Civil Rights: 'Black Power!'" *Newsweek*, June 27, 1966.

"Civil Rights: Heat on Highway 51." *Time*, June 17, 1966.

"Civil Rights: The New Racism." *Time*, July 1, 1966.

Cook, K. W. "King Leads Marchers on Meredith's Route." *Memphis Press-Scimitar*, June 8, 1966.

"The 'Death' Blunder." *Time*, June 17, 1966.

Eagles, Charles W. *The Price of Defiance: James Meredith and the Integration of Ole Miss*. Chapel Hill: The University of North Carolina Press, 2009.

Fleming, Karl. "'He Shot Me Like a Goddam Rabbit'." *Newsweek*, June 20, 1966.

Fletcher, Frank. "Judge Rules Against Norvell," *Memphis Press-Scimitar*, November 21, 1966.

"Friends and Foes of the Marchers." *New York Times*, June 19, 1966.

Fruhman, Barton. "Rights Leaders Flay Emotions." Memphis *Commercial Appeal*, June 8, 1966.

Glaude, Eddie S., Jr. *Democracy in Black: How Race Still Enslaves the American Soul*. New York: Crown Publishers, 2016.

Goudsouzian, Aram. *Down to the Crossroads: Civil Rights, Black Power, and the Meredith March Against Fear*. New York: Farrar, Straus and Giroux, 2014.

———. "Three Weeks in Mississippi: James Meredith, Aubrey Norvell, and the Politics of Bird Shot." *Journal of the Historical Society*, Vol. XI, no. 1 (March 2011).

"Governor Reduces State Guard for Marchers." Memphis *Commercial Appeal*, June 17, 1966.

"Grenada Reneged, King Charges." *Memphis Press-Scimitar*, July 8, 1966.

Hamilton, Roy B. and Brown Alan Flynn. "Rights Leaders March." *Memphis Press-Scimitar*, June 8, 1966.

Hampton, Henry, and Steve Fayer. *Voices of Freedom: An Oral History of the Civil Rights Movement From the 1950s Through the 1980s*. New York: Bantam, 1991.

James Howard Meredith Collection. University of Mississippi, Department of Archives and Special Collections.

Johnson, James Weldon. *Lift Every Voice and*

Sing: A Pictorial Tribute to the Negro National Anthem. New York: Jump at the Sun, 2000.

Joseph, Peniel E. *Stokely: A Life.* New York: Basic Civitas, Perseus Books Group, 2014.

———. *Waiting 'Til the Midnight Hour: A Narrative History of Black People in America.* New York: Henry Holt and Company, 2006.

Kasher, Steven. *The Civil Rights Movement: A Photographic History, 1954–68.* New York: Abbeville Press, 2000.

Kifner, John. "Rights Leaders Plan to Take Up Meredith's March in Mississippi." *New York Times,* June 7, 1966.

King, Martin Luther, Jr. "Nonviolence: The Only Road to Freedom." *Ebony,* October 1966.

———. *Where Do We Go from Here: Chaos or Community?* Boston: Beacon Press, 1968.

Lambert, Frank. *The Battle of Ole Miss: Civil Rights* v. *States' Rights.* New York: Oxford University Press, 2010.

Lawson, James. Author interview, Los Angeles, California, March 8, 2012.

———. Interviews with Memphis Search for Meaning Committee, Memphis, Tennessee, 1969.

———. "The Meredith March ... and Tomorrow." *Concern,* July 15, 1966.

Lester, Julius. *Look Out, Whitey! Black Power's Gon' Get Your Mama!* New York: Dial Press, 1968.

Loewen, James W. "Why Do People Believe Myths About the Confederacy? Because Our Textbooks and Monuments Are Wrong." *Washington Post,* July 1, 2015.

"March in Delta Marked by Petty Provocations." *Jackson Clarion-Ledger,* June 18, 1966.

"The March in Mississippi." CBS Special Report, June 26, 1966.

"The March—In Step and Out." *Newsweek,* July 4, 1966.

"The March Meredith Began." *Newsweek,* June 20, 1966.

Martin, Jack. "King Denounces 'Invisible Wall,' Black Power." Memphis *Commercial Appeal,* September 10, 1966.

McFadden, Robert D. "First Murder Charge in '64 Civil Rights Killings of 3." *New York Times,* January 7, 2005.

Meet the Press. NBC production transcript, Vol. 10, no. 25, June 19, 1966, Washington, D.C.

Memphis Search for Meaning Committee records, Preservation and Special Collections Department, University Libraries, University of Memphis.

"Meredith Assailant Is Free." *New York Times,* June 30, 1968.

"Meredith Begins Jackson March." Memphis *Commercial Appeal,* June 6, 1966.

"Meredith Sets Walk to Help Negro Vote." *New York Times,* May 23. 1966.

"Meredith to Start March on Sunday." Memphis *Commercial Appeal,* June 1, 1966.

"Meredith to Start Mississippi March." *New York Times,* June 1, 1966.

"Meredith Shuns Rally." *New York Times,* June 25, 1966.

Meredith, James. Author interview, Jackson, Mississippi, April 7, 2012.

———. "Big Changes Are Coming." *Saturday Evening Post.* August 13, 1966.

———. "A Challenge to Change." *Newsweek,* October 6, 1997.

———. *A Mission From God: A Memoir and Challenge for America.* New York: Atria Books, 2012 (with William Doyle).

———. *Three Years in Mississippi.* Bloomington: Indiana University Press, 1966.

"Mississippi: Br'er Fox." *Time,* July 24, 1966.

Mitchell, Jerry. "KKK Killed Ben Chester White, Hoping to Lure & Kill MLK." *Jackson Clarion-Ledger,* June 10, 2014.

"Negroes' Rally Tests Granada." *Memphis Press-Scimitar,* July 9, 1966.

"PBJ Urges Ignoring Marchers." *Jackson Daily News.* June 26, 1966.

Plona, Stanley. (Diary entries made during March Against Fear.) Memphis Search for Meaning Committee records, Preservation and Special Collections Department, University Libraries, University of Memphis.

Randal, Jonathan. "Onward They March and It's No Fun." *New York Times*, June 18, 1966.

Reed, Roy. "Meredith Begins Mississippi Walk to Combat Fear." *New York Times*, June 6, 1966.

———. "Meredith Is Shot in Back on Walk Into Mississippi." *New York Times*, June 7, 1966.

———. "Meredith Regrets He Was Not Armed." *New York Times*, June 8, 1966.

———. "Philadelphia, Miss., Whites and Negroes Trade Shots." *New York Times*, June 22, 1966.

Roberts, Gene. "Marchers Stage Mississippi Rally." *New York Times*, June 18, 1966.

———. "Meredith Hailed at Rally at Mississippi's Capitol." *New York Times*, June 27, 1966.

———. "Meredith Leads the March on Eve of Rally in Jackson." *New York Times*, June 26, 1966.

———. "Mississippi March Puts Rights Drive Into Evangelist Phase." *New York Times*, June 19, 1966.

———. "Mississippi Police Use Gas to Rout Rights Campers." *New York Times*, June 24, 1966.

———. "Mississippi Reduces Police Protection for Marchers." *New York Times*, June 17, 1966.

———. "Mississippi Shuns March Incidents." *New York Times*, June 16, 1966.

———. "Negroes Win Voting Gains on Stop in Grenada, Miss." *New York Times*, June 15, 1966.

———. "Troopers Shove Group Resuming Meredith March." *New York Times*, June 8, 1966.

Roberts, Gene, and Hank Klibanoff. *The Race Beat: The Press, the Civil Rights Struggle, and the Awakening of a Nation.* New York: Alfred A. Knopf, 2006.

Ronald "Butch" Alford Collection. Preservation and Special Collections Department, University Libraries, University of Memphis.

Rose, Mary. "Ignore Rabble, Writer Urges" (letter to the editor). *Jackson Clarion-Ledger*, June 24, 1966.

Schuessler, Jennifer. "Reconstruction, Reconstructed." *New York Times*, August 25, 2015.

Seeger, Pete, and Bob Reiser. *Everybody Says Freedom: A History of the Civil Rights Movement in Songs and Pictures.* New York: W. W. Norton & Company, 1989.

Sokol, Jason. *There Goes My Everything: White Southerners in the Age of Civil Rights, 1945–1975.* New York: Alfred A. Knopf, 2006.

"Suspect Admits He Shot Meredith." *New York Times*, November 22, 1966.

"Tactics of March Disturb Meredith." *New York Times*, June 16, 1966.

"The Talk of the Town." *New Yorker*, July 16, 1966. (Unsigned text by Renata Adler.)

"Though the Heavens Fall." *Time*, October 12, 1962.

The Time Has Come (1964–1966), from *Eyes on the Prize, America's Civil Rights Movement*, Vol. 4. A production of Blackside, 1990. Transcript available online through the *American Experience*.

"A Verdict in Mississippi." *New York Times* (editorial), June 23, 2005.

von Hoffman, Nicholas. "'Golly, This Is History'; and They March On." *Washington Post*, June 10, 1966.

———. "March Enters Jackson Amid Hostility." *Washington Post*, June 27, 1966.

———. "The Marchers Look for Luck on Rt. 7." *Washington Post*, June 16, 1966.

"A Walk in the South to Conquer Old Fears." *Life*, June 17, 1966.

Watson, Bruce. *Freedom Summer: The Savage Season of 1964 That Made Mississippi Burn and Made America a Democracy.* New York: Penguin Books, 2011.

Wilkerson, Isabel. *The Warmth of Other Suns: The Epic Story of America's Great Migration.* New York: Vintage Books, 2011.

PHOTOGRAPHY CREDITS

Abbreviations used below are as follows: **AP**—Associated Press; **Fitch**—Photo by Bob Fitch, Bob Fitch Photography Archive, courtesy of the Department of Special Collections, Stanford University Libraries; **Peppler**—Photo by Jim Peppler, Jim Peppler *Southern Courier* Photograph Collection, courtesy of the Alabama Department of Archives and History, Montgomery, Alabama; **UM**—Memphis *Press-Scimitar* collections, courtesy of the Preservation and Special Collections Department, University Libraries, University of Memphis; **UPI**—United Press International.

Front cover, Matt Herron/Take Stock/The Image Works; 2–3, Matt Herron/Take Stock/The Image Works; 7, Jack Thornell/AP; 8, William Leaptrott/UM; 10, UM; 11, UM; 16, James R. Reid/UM; 20, Rolls Press/Popperfoto/Getty; 22, Lynn Pelham/Getty; 25, Tom Barber/UM; 26, Tom Barber/Getty; 30, William Leaptrott/UM; 34, Fitch; 38, Peppler; 43, UPI/UM; 45, Peppler; 46, Peppler; 50, Bettmann/Getty; 53, Bettmann/Getty; 54, UPI/UM; 55, Fitch; 59, Tom Barber/UM; 60–61, Fitch; 64, Fitch; 67, Fitch; 70, Peppler; 73, Rolls Press/Popperfoto/Getty; 75, Fitch; 78, Bettmann/Getty; 80, Fitch; 84, Peppler; 88, Harry Benson/Getty; 94–95, Bettmann/Getty; 96, AP; 97, AP; 99, Peppler; 102, Peppler; 105, Dozier Mobley/Getty; 107, Fitch; 110, Fitch; 113, Dozier Mobley/Getty; 114, Peppler; 118, AP; 121, Douglas Glynn/Getty; 122, Fitch; 123, UPI/UM.

CITATIONS

The following names have been abbreviated: Stokely Carmichael (SC), Martin Luther King, Jr. (MLK), Floyd McKissick (FM), and James H. Meredith (JHM).

HALF-TITLE PAGE

1, MLK: "There is nothing ... marching feet." (Fruhman).

PROLOGUE—A TREMOR

6, JHM: "Get a car and get me in it." (Reed, "Meredith Is Shot in Back on Walk Into Mississippi"); 7, Hospital resident in Memphis: "If he had been ... and sent him home." (Ronald "Butch" Alford Collection).

CHAPTER 1—WILD IDEAS

8, JHM: "I wanted to give hope ... myself for 16 years." (James Howard Meredith Collection); 15, JHM: "just operating on its own accord." (Meredith, author interview, April 7, 2012); 17, JHM: "There are a million Negroes ... take care of me." (Reed, "Meredith Begins Mississippi Walk to Combat Fear"); 18, Sudanese village chief: "We shall arrive." (Burks); 18, JHM: "I was ecstatic." (Meredith, author interview, April 7, 2012); 18, JHM: "day for Negro men being cowards is over." (James Howard Meredith Collection); 19, Julius Lester: "With this announcement ... announced his death." (Lester: 3); 19, Nicholas Katzenbach: "I don't think it's going to amount to much." (Goudsouzian, 2014: 8).

CHAPTER 2—REACTIONS

20, James Lawson: "I think the entire incident ... what might come of it?" (Lawson, "The Meredith March ... and Tomorrow"); 25, Roy Wilkins: "another country" and "We are going to show ... the 50 states." (Fruhman); 26, SC: "really make this the last march." (Goudsouzian, 2014: 60); 27, SC: "that cat Johnson." (Branch, 2006: 477); 28, JHM: "I shall return to my divine responsibility" and "and we shall reach our destination." (Goudsouzian, 2011: 49); 28, JHM: "I could have knocked ... had I been prepared."

(James Howard Meredith Collection); 28, JHM: "Who the hell ever said ... rest of my life in Mississippi." (Reed, "Meredith Regrets He Was Not Armed"); 29, FM: "The shooting of James Meredith ... way of life in Mississippi." (Kifner); 29, Russell H. Barrett: "Mississippi is emotionally ... risk of verbal or physical attack." (James Howard Meredith Collection).

CHAPTER 3—REVIVED

30, MLK: "Marching feet announce ... change is missing also." (King, "Nonviolence: The Only Road to Freedom"); 33, Armistead Phipps: "This is the greatest thing ... won't be afraid to vote anymore." (Goudsouzian, 2014: 52); 33, MLK: "His death means ... overworked and underpaid." (von Hoffman, "'Golly, This Is History'; and They March On"); 36, Eddie Ford: "When I saw them ... wanted my freedom." (Goudsouzian, 2014: 70); 37, Recruitment letter: "If you and enough of your ... that by doing so he risks his life." (Memphis Search for Meaning Committee records); 37, White planter: "To expect a group ... that's asking too much of human nature." (Sokol: 110).

CHAPTER 4—DELTA BOUND

38, Joseph Lee: "There are things ... why we did them *then*." ("The Talk of the Town"); 41, Ben Chester White: "Oh, Lord, what have I done to deserve this?" (Mitchell); 42, MLK: "This was a man who was not afraid." (Branch, 2006: 478); 43, Mississippi state patrol officer: "a great assembly of kooks." (Branch, 2006: 483); 46, James Lawson: "The state provided ... protection for segregation against us." (Lawson, "The Meredith March ... and Tomorrow"); 46, Stanley Plona: "It's typical 'Freedom Movement' organization ... everything manages to get done." (Plona: 2); 47, Thomas Tatum: "When you have a custom ... it's hard to shake." (Goudsouzian, 2014: 131); 49, P. L. Elion: "I think the daylight's breakin'." (Goudsouzian, 2014: 56); 49, Editorial: "If we remain segregationists ... restoring our Southern way of life." (Goudsouzian, 2014: 111–112).

CHAPTER 5—BLACK POWER

50, MLK: "This is a movement ... free him of his fear." (Goudsouzian, 2014: 86); 51, Chant: "Come on over, brother, come on over, brother." (Roberts, "Negroes Win Voting Gains on Stop in Grenada, Miss."); 51, Tessie McCain: "I was just looking" and "and all of a sudden I was marching." (Roberts, "Negroes Win Voting Gains on Stop in Grenada, Miss."); 52, Robert Green: "We're tired of seeing rebel flags" and "Give me the flag of the United States, the flag of freedom!" (Roberts, "Negroes Win Voting Gains on Stop in Grenada, Miss."); 52, Robert Green: "We want Brother Jefferson ... never rise again." ("Mississippi: Br'er Fox"); 52, Robert Green: "This is not the Confederacy, this is America!" ("Civil Rights: 'Black Power!'"); 53, City Manager John McEachin: "All we want ... out of here." (Goudsouzian, 2014: 120); 54, Lewis Johnson: "All of a sudden ... courage, defiance, outspokenness." (Goudsouzian, 2014: 119); 55, Governor Paul Johnson: "turned into a voter registration campaign." ("Governor Reduces State Guard for Marchers"); 55, Governor Paul Johnson: "We are not ... a group of showmen." ("Governor Reduces State Guard for Marchers); 56, Charles McLaurin: "It was like the messiah walking through the community." (Goudsouzian, 2014: 179); 56, Girl in Cleveland: "I want to go with him." ("The Talk of the Town"); 56, White man in Charleston: "Get out of here ... and get out fast." (Goudsouzian, 2014: 130); 56, JHM: "There seems to be a good bit of show going on down there." (von Hoffman, "The Marchers Look for Luck on Rt. 7"); 56, JHM: "is not a testing ground ... strengths of their leaders." ("Tactics of March Disturb Meredith"); 56, JHM: "gain respect for the Negro." (von Hoffman, "The Marchers Look for Luck on Rt. 7"); 57, Letter signed A.O.: "You say you don't believe ... we will be ready." (James Howard Meredith Collection); 57, Letter from Anne Wyne: "ashamed to belong to a race who believes itself superior." (James Howard Meredith Collection); 57, Letter from Cynthia: "My classmates ... hope your back gets well." (James Howard Meredith Collection); 57, Letter from Carlos: "I hope you help people to not make violence." (James Howard Meredith Collection); 57, Letter from William: "Next time make sure you have a gun on you." (James Howard Meredith Collection); 58, Robert Green: "We've had enough of that!" and "I want this stopped." ("Arrest 3 Marchers Then Open Up Park"); 59, SC: "We'll put them up anyway." (Roberts, "Mississippi Reduces Police Protection for Marchers"); 59, B.A. Hammond: "You are not putting those tents up here." ("Arrest 3 Marchers Then Open Up Park"); 59, SC: "We are raising these tents." ("Arrest 3 Marchers Then Open Up Park"); 59, B.A. Hammond: "Frank, if he puts ... arrest him." ("Arrest 3 Marchers Then Open Up Park"); 61, Robert Green: "Are you with us?" (Goudsouzian, 2014: 141); 63, African-American woman from Drew: "If you think he's wrong ... sold like cattle." (Goudsouzian, 2014: 130); 63, Greenwood segregationists: "We will live here ... with your remains." (Goudsouzian, 2014: 149).

CHAPTER 6—EARTHQUAKE

64, SC: "Each time the people ... they were steaming." (Carmichael: 5); 66, SC: "This is the 27th time I have been arrested ... start saying now is 'black power.'" (Roberts and Klibanoff: 399); 66, SC & chant: "Don't be ashamed" and "We want black power" (repeated) ("The March in Mississippi"); 66, SC: "That's right ... We've done nothing but beg." ("The March in Mississippi"); 66, SC: "We've got to stop begging and take power." (Goudsouzian, 2014: 143); 66, SC: "Ain't nothin' wrong ... That's what we want—black power!" (Goudsouzian, 2014: 143); 66, SC: "It's time we stand up ... get rid of the dirt and the mess. ("The March in Mississippi"); 66, SC: "Now from now on ... you know what to tell them. ("The March in Mississippi"); 66–67, Call and response: "What do you want?" and "Black Power!" ("The March in Mississippi"); 67, SC: "That's what we're gonna get." ("The March in Mississippi"); 68, Bob Fitch: "We're watching history." (Goudsouzian, 2014: 143); 68, MLK: "too polite" and "just didn't feel like Mississippi." (Branch, 2006: 486); 68, MLK: "Power is the ability to make ... is to be voters." ("March in Delta Marked by Petty Provocations"); 68, MLK: "When we get this ... society of brotherhood." (Roberts, "Marchers Stage Mississippi Rally"); 69, Leon Hall: "We do need black ... the white folks like they done to us." (Goudsouzian, 2014: 162); 69, James Phipps: "If you say a couple of radical words ... Northern white man." (Roberts, "Mississippi March Puts Rights Drive Into Evangelist Phase"); 69, David Dawley: "Suddenly the happy feeling ... we don't need you.'" (Hampton and Feyer: 290); 69, Dick Reavis: "seemed like ... what the movement had been about." (Goudsouzian, 2014: 98); 69, Malcolm X: "Give it to us now ... and that's not fast enough." (Joseph, 2006: 102); 71, John Lewis: "If it hadn't been for the media ... a choir without a song." (Roberts and Klibanoff: 407); 71–72, Renata Adler: "Perhaps the reason ... the props are becoming stereotyped." ("The Talk of the Town"); 72, *Time*: "a racist philosophy." ("Civil Rights: The New Racism"); 72, *Newsweek*: "battle cry of racial alienation." ("Civil Rights: 'Black Power!'"); 72, Taylor Branch: "seized on" and "it essentially says ... are about to make war.'" (*Citizen King*); 73, Julius Lester: "All the whites wanted to know ... The nation was hysterical." (Lester: 98); 73, Aram Goudsouzian: "Of course they chanted ... and they had no power." (Goudsouzian, 2014: 163); 73, Stanley Plona: "Nobody in camp ... the whole thing was all about." (Plona: 11); 73–74, SC: "I don't think ... they aren't black." (Roberts and Klibanoff: 400); 74, SC: "The Student Nonviolent Coordinating Committee is speaking ... people who oppose that are anti-black." ("The March in Mississippi"); 74, SC: "I stand mute." ("The March in Mississippi"); 74, Elizabeth Sunderland: "juicy quotes. Be a little more boring." (Goudsouzian, 2014: 135); 76, MLK: "I don't care ... still be the last one to cry against it." (Goudsouzian, 2014: 168); 76, SC: "That doesn't mean we're anti-white" and "We are just developing pride." (Joseph, 2014: 116); 76, SC: "The only way ... counties to institute justice." (*Citizen King*); 76, FM: "I think it scared people ... a violent instrument accompanying it." (Hampton and Fayer: 292); 77, SC: "It is time to stop being ashamed ... *she is beautiful.*" ("The Talk of the Town"); 77, White customer in a Grenada barbershop: "They can pass ... mow 'em down." (von Hoffman, "The Marchers Look for Luck on Rt. 7").

CHAPTER 7—WHITE RAGE

78, Song lyrics: "Ain't Gonna Let Nobody Turn Me 'Round." (Seeger and Reiser: 74–75); 79, Fannie Lou Hamer: "The people are moving with us now" and "And even those ... for the first time." (Goudsouzian, 2014: 130); 80, Stanley Plona: "The conflict quite obviously wasn't going to be solved yet." (Plona: 8); 80, Tommy Johnson: "A kitty cat!" (Goudsouzian, 2014: 162); 80, Marchers: "A little rest!" (Goudsouzian, 2014: 166); 81, JHM: "I think that the nonviolence is ... can ever go far enough." (*Meet the Press*, June 19, 1966: 2); 82, SC: "deliberately decided ... a stand on black power." (King, 1968: 31); 82, MLK: "I have been used before" and "One more time won't hurt." (King, 1968: 31); 82, MLK: "Because Stokely Carmichael chose ... helped Mississippi get off the hook somewhat." (Kasher: 197); 83, Philadelphia woman: "I wouldn't dirty my Goddamned car with you black bastards!" (Reed, "Philadelphia, Miss., Whites and

Negroes Trade Shots"); 85, Roy Reed: *"This is the day he will die."* (Goudsouzian, 2014: 174); 85–86, MLK: "I believe in my heart ... at this moment." (Reed: "Philadelphia, Miss., Whites and Negroes Trade Shots"); 86, White boy in Philadelphia, Mississippi: "They're right behind you!" ("The March—In Step and Out"); 86, MLK: "We are not afraid ... have to kill all of us." (Reed, "Philadelphia, Miss., Whites and Negroes Trade Shots"); 86, Psalm 23, excerpts. (Bible, King James Version); 86, MLK: "This is a terrible town ... a complete reign of terror here." (Reed: "Philadelphia, Miss., Whites and Negroes Trade Shots"); 87, MLK: "I am not afraid of any man ... I am not afraid of any man." (Reed. "Philadelphia, Miss., Whites and Negroes Trade Shots"); 87, Heckler in Philadelphia, Mississippi: "Hey, Luther! ... and prove it." (Reed. "Philadelphia, Miss., Whites and Negroes Trade Shots").

CHAPTER 8—SUPREMACY

88, FM: "They don't call it *white* power ... get us some *black* power." ("The Talk of the Town"); 90, MLK: "Somebody said tonight ... freedom by ourselves." (Goudsouzian, 2014: 180) 90, MLK: "The weakness of violence ... they can't stop it." (Goudsouzian, 2014: 181); 90, MLK: "I'm disturbed about a strange theory ... Oh, no." ("The March in Mississippi"); 90, Crowd member: "Oh, no!" ("The March in Mississippi"); 90–91, MLK: "That I will not do ... evil throughout our civilization." ("The March in Mississippi"); 91, MLK: "I am sick and tired of power ... I'm not going to use violence no matter who says it." ("The March in Mississippi"); 92, SC: "They said we couldn't ... going to do it *now*!" (Goudsouzian, 2014: 197); 92, Robert Gorza, Canton city attorney: "You will not be allowed ... placed under arrest." ("The March—In Step and Out"); 92, FM: "When we say lock arms ... sit down." (Goudsouzian, 2014: 198); 93, MLK: "I want to get this over ... if they start arresting us!" (*The Time Has Come*); 93, Chant: "We're gonna pitch ... the tents!" ("The March in Mississippi"); 93, Chant: "Freedom! Freedom!" ("The March in Mississippi"); 93, FM: "Take out your handkerchiefs ... over your face." (Roberts: "Mississippi Police Use Gas to Rout Rights Campers"); 93, Shouts: "No, no!" and "Freedom!" and "We're gonna pitch the tents!" ("The March in Mississippi"); 93, MLK: "Nobody leave ... stand our ground." (Branch, 2006: 490); 93, Jo Freeman: "My whole body felt ... inhaling molten steel." (Goudsouzian, 2014: 201); 94, Reporter: "At one point, an eerie silence ... clubbing fallen marchers." ("Civil Rights: The New Racism"); 94, Arlie Schardt, *Time*: "It was like a scene of hell." (Goudsouzian, 2014: 200); 95, Robert Gorza, Canton city attorney: "Suppose they got away ... to take City Hall next." (Roberts: "Mississippi Police Use Gas to Rout Rights Campers"); 95, Governor Paul Johnson: "the humane thing to do." (Goudsouzian, 2014: 205); 96, Paul Good: "were not arresting, they were punishing." (Kasher: 213); 96, SC: "Don't make your stand here ...see any more people shot." ("The Talk of the Town"); 96, FM: "I'm tired of having to *negotiate* our Constitutional *rights*." ("The Talk of the Town"); 96, MLK: "Oh, not at all" and "How could we ... police force like that?" ("The March in Mississippi"); 96, MLK: The government has got to ... keep people nonviolent." (Goudsouzian, 2014: 206); 98, Lyndon B. Johnson: "We are not interested in ... with a small 'd.'" (Joseph, 2014: 127–128); 100, Harry Reasoner: "police protection was much better, but the jeering was worse." ("The March in Mississippi"); 100, MLK: "We were brutalized ... going to have our freedom." (Branch, 2006: 491); 100, James Lawson: "turned their bayonets toward us." (Lawson, author interview, March 8, 2012); 101, White woman: "Can't you see ... Can't you see it?" (Roberts, "Mississippi Police Use Gas to Rout Rights Campers"); 101, Canton policeman: "I couldn't see it, friend, I couldn't see it." (Roberts, "Mississippi Police Use Gas to Rout Rights Campers").

CHAPTER 9—REUNITED

102, JHM: "The state of Mississippi ... had to demonstrate that it was master." (James Howard Meredith Collection); 104, JHM: I don't know ... smells to me." ("Meredith Shuns Rally"); 106, Charles Snodgrass: "Are you armed?" (Goudsouzian, 2014: 223); 106, JHM: "He has given me his word." (Roberts, "Meredith Leads the March on Eve of Rally in Jackson"); 107, MLK: "I hope this is in light of what you wanted." (Goudsouzian, 2014: 223); 107, JHM: "This is the most beautiful thing I have seen in a long time." (Goudsouzian, 2014: 223); 108, Invitation: "Everyone is invited" and "the basic philosophy of nonviolence." (Goudsouzian, 2014: 227); 108, Dick Gregory: "When y'all get to saying it ... you're saying 'Black Powder'!" (Goudsouzian, 2014: 226); 108, MLK: "I'm sorry, y'all. James Brown is on. I'm gone." (Branch, 2006: 492); 109, Annie

Devine: "We are not going to stay ignorant, and backward, and scared." ("The Talk of the Town"); 109, Mary Rose, letter to the editor: "Aren't we civilized enough to ignore these rabble rousers?" (Rose).

CHAPTER 10—FINALE

110, Song lyrics: "Sing a song full ... victory is won." (Johnson); 111, Singers: "We've got the light of freedom." (Goudsouzian, 2014: 236); 112, Police officer: "Goddamn you ... head off." (von Hoffman, "March Enters Jackson Amid Hostility"); 112, White onlookers: "Shoot! Shoot!" (von Hoffman, "March Enters Jackson Amid Hostility"); 114, SC: "Bring those folks ... up front here." (von Hoffman, "March Enters Jackson Amid Hostility"); 115, JHM: "the system of white supremacy will reign no longer." ("The March in Mississippi"); 115, JHM speech: "I want to thank all the people ... I thank you all." ("The March in Mississippi"); 115, SC: "We have to stop being ashamed of being black!" and "We have to move ... ever be afraid!" (Goudsouzian, 2014: 242); 115, SC: "must build a power base ... mess with us!" (Roberts, "Meredith Hailed at Rally at Mississippi's Capitol"); 115, FM: "It's just an adjective inserted before a noun." (Goudsouzian, 2014: 242–243); 116, MLK: "This will be the day ... of man *as* man!" (Goudsouzian, 2014: 243); 117, Monroe Williams: "If my daddy had done this ... doing it for the children." (Roberts, "Meredith Hailed at Rally at Mississippi's Capitol"); 117, Governor Paul Johnson: "I urge all of our citizens ... in this great state." ("PBJ Urges Ignoring Marchers").

CHAPTER 11—AFTERSHOCKS

118, JHM: "You who live in the North ... And the hour is getting late." (Meredith, "Big Changes Are Coming"); 120, David Dawley: "We listened to what SNCC was saying ... that was Vietnam." (Hampton and Feyer: 294); 122, MLK: "It is necessary ... a cry of disappointment." (King, 1968: 32); 122, MLK: "For 12 years I ... a frustrating nightmare." (King, 1968: 45); 123, JHM: "I had to continue ... I was not afraid." (Goudsouzian, 2014: 251); 124, JHM: "'Mississippi' is the most powerful word in the English language." (Meredith, author interview, April 7, 2012); 124, Jack Cauthen: "there hadn't been no pellets ... was shot, no sir." (Goudsouzian, 2014: 222); 124, O. D. Crawford: "There actually never was ... during that time." (Goudsouzian, 2014: 205); 126, MLK: "Only a refusal to hate ... change in our lives." (King, "Nonviolence: The Only Road to Freedom"); 127, MLK: "I'm convinced that Mississippi will never be the same again." (Goudsouzian, 2014: 121); 127, Sheriff's deputy: "After they leave, everything will be the same again." (Goudsouzian, 2014: 122).

CLOSING QUOTATION

144, SC: "For racism to die, a totally different America must be born." (Carmichael: 6).

INDEX

Illustrations are indicated by **boldface.** If Illustrations are included within a page span, the entire span is **boldface.**